1.50

COOKING FOR CROWDS

DRAWINGS BY

Edward Koren

COOKING FOR CROWDS

MERRY WHITE

BASIC BOOKS, INC.

Publishers   NEW YORK

Library of Congress Cataloging in Publication Data

White, Merry, 1941-
    Cooking for crowds.

    Includes index.
    1. Cookery.   I.   Title.
TX820.W48   641.5'7   74-79051
ISBN 0-465-01426-7

74 75 76 77 78   10 9 8 7 6 5 4 3 2

Contents

Introduction   *vii*

Pots, Pans, and Utensils   *xiii*

Herbs and Spices   *xvii*

Conversion   *xx*

Acknowledgments   *xxi*

Soups and Starters   *1*

Main Dishes   *45*

Vegetables and Side Dishes   *119*

Desserts   *145*

List of Illustrations   *177*

Index   *179*

Introduction

I was trying to live on my writing while going to graduate school when I discovered cooking for pay. I was a passable cook with some adventurousness, but I had never cooked for more than a conventional eight-person dinner party, and that in my own kitchen. I was—and sometimes still am—terrified at the thought of cooking for twenty to fifty people at a time. Somehow I managed—and now I even enjoy it. This book is the result of the pleasure and the terror, and the sometimes uneasy accommodation between the two.

The great lesson was that I can do it: I can cook a dinner for an Eminent Person and assembled guests, write a term paper, and take my daughter to her ballet classes and back. I wouldn't do large-crowd cookery every day, but I've discovered enough shortcuts and efficiencies to make it work.

I can recall meals I've catered that almost blew my cool, such as the one for Lord Harlech and twenty-five others (individual shrimp quiches, *saltimbocca*, asparagus with hollandaise, *pilau*, salad, and *coeurs à la crème* with strawberries), which was somehow reheated over two hot-plate burners at the Kennedy Institute of Politics. It worked, but I wouldn't repeat it.

The prospect of serving food to crowds usually drives most people to a professional caterer. This is an expensive and unnecessary expedient. In fact, one person with an ordinary kitchen and ordinary tools can, with little money and anxiety, produce a full meal for fifty—and still enjoy the party.

Even better, the foods that are served can be as interesting and elegant, as exotic and original, as anything you might serve to a dinner party of six. You need not rely on the bland clichés of the catered dinner, the Jell-o salads, chicken à la king, and other insults to the palate. Fear of offending motivates too many menus; the lowest common denominator of taste is much higher than one might think. When I first began to cook for large groups, I thought I had to make the predictably dull food typical of catering. The guests and I were both bored, so I was delighted to find that more adventurous dishes pleased everyone.

"Exotic" foods are not only interesting, they also provide an atmosphere of informal adventure, much the best atmosphere for eating. Most of the meals I serve are buffet style, which helps create an atmosphere of informality. "Serving" is not something I enjoy doing, but it needn't be an unpleasant chore when the meal is informal and exciting.

I cooked for the Center for West European Studies at Harvard University for a year, and I found that it is not an overwhelming task to do alone. During the school term, there is a luncheon for fifty people every Friday and occasional dinners for invited guests. My job was to prepare the Friday luncheons and the often weekly dinners, and my audience was a very sophisticated group of faculty, graduate students, and guests. With adequate storage space, it is possible—albeit hectic—to do a dinner for twenty and a luncheon for fifty within a two-day period. Be willing to cook for numbers you never considered before. Cooking for fifty is not more difficult, only more time-consuming, than cooking for twenty; cooking for twenty takes only slightly more time than cooking for ten.

In learning to cook for crowds, I have developed some efficiencies, some tricks to bolster my confidence. For instance, if I am nervous about a meal, I choose dishes that can be made at least one day in advance. Most of the dishes in this book fall into this category. You can usually arrange it so that all you need to do before the meal is perhaps to heat up a casserole, toss a salad (the greens can be washed, dried, torn, and packaged in plastic earlier), slice bread, and perhaps whip cream for a dessert.

Start as far ahead as you can without dragging out the job too much. The first thing to do is make up the menu and check to be sure that you haven't planned a completely beige meal (as I did once, until I changed the dessert to chocolate and introduced a green salad), or one in which there are too many last minute jobs. Serve only a few dishes and have them be good ones: a magnificent *couscous*, salad, and fruit is more than enough.

Check to see that you do not have to heat up several things at different oven temperatures at the same time. Decide which dishes can be made one or two days ahead and make a master shopping list, with separate lists for the ahead-of-time dishes. Plan to have enough refrigerator and freezer space to store ingredients and finished dishes. (I have indicated when a dish does not need refrigeration.) In cold weather I use back hall storage space to keep fresh produce and finished (but not too perishable) dishes cool. I also borrow space in my neighbor's refrigerator, for which I hereby give thanks.

If you expand recipes from other cookbooks, you must make allowances beyond simply multiplying ingredients. Some spices are powerful enough that you should not simply multiply them as you might be multiplying everything else—use the measurements in this book as a guideline for similar recipes.

Some enlarged recipes won't bake like the originals. It is better to make eight standard-sized pies than four oversized ones, because the timing in the oven can be more accurate. If you have very large pans, they will need more time in the oven, and perhaps be baked at a lower temperature, so that the edges don't burn before the center cooks. Crowding also changes the timing. If you have six pies in the oven, they will take more time than two. And it is better in baking, always, to use the same depth pan for a large amount as for a small amount, rather than a deeper one.

The recipes that follow are not expensive to prepare. The same meals from a caterer, if you could get them, would cost at least four times the amount you will pay cooking by yourself (not counting your labor). The markup on retailed prepared food is enormous, as you can see from restaurant menus. A simple luncheon for fifty, consisting of a casserole, salad, French bread and butter, nonalcoholic beverage, dessert, and coffee to follow, will cost you approximately $70.00 in ingredients, or less if you use inexpensive recipes such as Swedish Meatballs (page 81), Portuguese Sausage Casserole (page 73), Joy Walker's Chili (page 69), or Moussaka (page 87). A similar three-course meal from a caterer would be at least $6.00 a person.

Some of the most successful "crowd" meals I've served were nothing more than an inexpensive hearty soup, good hot bread, salad, and a dessert. Of course you should watch for specials on meats, and so on, and store them in the freezer if you have one.

It is important also to remember that celebratory dining does not require the most expensive cuts of meat; indeed, dishes like the ones in this book are better prepared with cheaper cuts. Save the tender fillet for a small dinner, when you can cook it in the few minutes it requires and when a waiting group will appreciate the care you have taken.

This book can be used in many ways. You can cook for a small group or family of 6, or larger groups of 12, 20, or 50 people. It is often a wise idea to try a recipe for 6 before you make it for 50. You will notice that in spicy dishes the "heat" is often slightly reduced in the amounts for 50: in such a large group, I find it better to play it safe.

Pots, Pans, and Utensils

I have no special kitchen for catering, and few special pots. The following hints give some ideas as to accommodations anyone might make for a large dinner.

First, obtain a large preserving kettle, usually quite inexpensive. I use two and they are suitable for many tasks: marinating meats, simmering chickens, mixing large quantities of dough or batter. If you are not going to invest in good, large catering pans, use heavy-duty foil roasting pans and foil pie tins. But for stews and other slow-cooking dishes, it is important to have a heavy pot.

If you plan much large-scale cooking, you should buy the largest porcelainized cast-iron Dutch oven you can afford. The Belgian and French are the best. Also, at junk shops and at some hardware stores you can find heavy cast-iron kettles, of the sort that used to hang in fireplaces. These need to be seasoned and carefully wiped after every use, but they cook evenly and well.

A large wooden tabletop is needed for chopping and slicing; small breadboards are not enough. If you haven't a top you can cut on, get a large, table-sized piece of hardwood to lay over your table.

One of the best places on which to work is the floor: if it is clean, it is a wonderful, flexible space. Cover it with a large sheet of vinyl first. When I was in Nepal my friends' cook worked on the floor, and it was much more convenient than juggling pots and pans and mounds of vegetables on small counter spaces. We had large round panniers on which the foods were spread, wooden slabs to cut on, and huge stone mortars for grinding and pounding. It was a liberating experience.

In the salad recipe on page 129 I describe my use of the floor (and bedsheets) for drying fifty people's worth of greens. Have a child or two help.

There are some special devices that should be described more fully. In the preparation of many Middle Eastern and Chinese dishes a steamer is needed. If, as is likely, you haven't a large one, you may improvise one as follows: Place a metal colander or very large sieve over a kettle one-third full of water in such a way that it is suspended over the water—you may have to tie it to the handles of the pot. For couscous or other fine ingredients to be steamed, line the colander with double cheesecloth first.

When you steam dumplings, like *momos*, place them on a greased plate in the steamer or colander, or construct the following:

HERBS AND SPICES

Herbs and Spices

Herbs and spices are important to almost every recipe in the book, and should not be dealt with offhandedly.

Herbs, the dried leaves of aromatic plants like thyme and basil, are most evanescent. Their flavor disappears with age, so you should make sure those you buy are fresh. You can grow most herbs easily in kitchen pots or gardens, and use them fresh or dry them. Finally, you should buy in small quantities to ensure freshness.

Spices are usually the seeds, bark, or seed cover of a plant, often sold ground. I usually buy them in the whole seed, in quantity, and grind them fresh as needed in the blender or with a mortar and pestle. Avoid buying large quantities of ground spices, as they quickly become just so much dust. One trick to bring out the flavor of spices is to heat them in a dry, heavy skillet (don't burn them!) before grinding.

A good selection to have around is:

HERBS

    dill (both weed and seed)
    thyme
    basil
    oregano
    tarragon
    mint
    rosemary
    bay leaves
    sage
    marjoram

SPICES

allspice (whole berry)

aniseed (whole)

caraway seeds

cardamom pods (the black seeds inside are used, the white pod discarded)

cayenne or whole dried red chilies

cinnamon (both stick and ground since it is hard to grind fine)

cloves (both whole and ground)

coriander (whole seed; sieve after grinding)

cumin (whole seed)

ginger (both ground and fresh; keep the fresh, peeled and left whole, in a glass jar, covered with dry sherry)

mustard seed (both whole and ground)

nutmeg (whole)

peppercorns (both black and white)

turmeric (ground)

SALTS

kosher salt

sea salt

Conversion

If you convert recipes from other books, note the following measurement equivalents:

3 teaspoons = 1 tablespoon
2 tablespoons = 1 fluid ounce
4 tablespoons = ¼ cup
12 tablespoons = ¾ cup
16 tablespoons = 1 cup
2 cups = 1 pint
2 pints = 1 quart
4 quarts = 1 gallon
1 cup granulated sugar = 7 oz
1 cup unsifted white flour = 5 oz
    or rye, or whole wheat
1 cup rice, uncooked = 7 oz

1 cup butter = 8 oz
1 cup bulghur wheat = 6 oz
    (cracked, for tabbouleh)
1 cup red lentils = 7 oz
1 cup shelled almonds = 4 oz
1 standard bottle of wine = 3½ cups
    or about 28 fluid oz
mixed dried fruit, 1 box = 1 lb
plain yogurt, small = 8 oz
        large = 2 lbs (32 oz)
cream cheese and farmer's cheese =
    8 oz per pkg

Acknowledgments

I would like to thank all those at the Center for West European Studies at Harvard for both encouraging and tolerating my experiments. In particular, I would like to thank Professor Stanley Hoffman, Abby Collins, Leonie Gordon, Peter Gourevitch, and all those who washed dishes, rushed hot food to tables, and cheerfully shared their food when too many people came.

I am grateful to Martha Lange who helped set up the first edition of the cookbook which the Center printed and distributed in Cambridge. Carol Bangs gave me space in her refrigerator, Lew Wurgaft scrubbed innumerable pots and pans and helped me through all the bad spots, and Jenny White chopped onions until the tears came. Thank you all.

SOUPS AND STARTERS

New Orleans Shrimp

This is an excellent cold appetizer: shrimp marinated in a spicy vinaigrette dressing, which must be served thoroughly chilled, perhaps on a bed of greens.

	6	12	20	50
olive oil	½ c	1 c	1⅔ c	3¼ c
garlic cloves, finely minced	2–3	4–6	7–9	10–12
small onions, finely chopped	2	4	7	10–12
raw shrimp, shelled and deveined	2 lbs	4 lbs	6⅔ lbs	15 lbs
scallions, finely chopped	6	12	20	30
lemon juice	½ c	1 c	1⅔ c	2½ c
salt	1 tsp	2 tsp	4 tsp	3 tbs
freshly ground black pepper	½ tsp	1 tsp	2 tsp	3 tsp
dry mustard	1 tsp	2 tsp	3 tsp	5 tsp
Tabasco, to taste, or	¼ tsp	½ tsp	¾ tsp	1¾ tsp
dried dillweed	2 tsp	4 tsp	2½ tbs	6 tbs

Heat one-third of the oil in a heavy skillet, add the minced garlic and onion, and cook, stirring occasionally, over a moderate flame for 10 minutes. Do not let brown. Add the shrimp and sauté for 5 to 7 minutes, still stirring, then remove from the heat and cool.

In a large bowl, combine the remaining oil, minced scallions, lemon juice, and seasonings. Add the shrimp mixture and toss thoroughly. Let marinate in the refrigerator for 6 to 24 hours, stirring occasionally. Serve quite cold, over ice if possible, with toothpicks.

Shrimp in Dill Pesto

Pesto is that green spaghetti sauce that gets its flavor and color from fresh basil. This fresh dill version is delicious on shrimp. Served cold on a lettuce "boat," this is an excellent first course.

A mixture of fresh dill and parsley may be used.

	6	12	20	50
white wine	½ c	1 c	1⅔ c	4 c
water	½ c	1 c	1⅔ c	4 c
peppercorns	6	12	20	50
bay leaves	1	2	3	8
thyme	½ tsp	1 tsp	1⅔ tsp	3¾ tsp
small onions	1	2	3	8
salt	1 tsp	2 tsp	3 tsp	8 tsp
raw shrimp, shelled and deveined	1 lb	2 lbs	3⅓ lbs	8 lbs
olive oil	¼ c	½ c	¾ c	2½ c
garlic cloves	4	7	12	26
fresh dill weed, roughly chopped	1½ c	3 c	5 c	12 c

Combine the wine, water, peppercorns, bay leaves, thyme, onions, and salt in a saucepan. Bring to a boil and simmer for 5 minutes. Add the shrimp and simmer only until the shrimp curl and turn pink, about 5 minutes. Remove the shrimp from the pan, then turn up the heat and reduce the liquid by half.

Make the pesto in batches by pouring the olive oil about ½ cup at a time into the blender. Add some of the garlic and dill to each batch and blend. Empty the blender into a large bowl as you go. Repeat until all the oil and dill and garlic are used up. When all is thick and smooth, stir the reduced cooking liquid into the bowl and beat hard until the pesto is creamy and smooth.

Put the shrimp in a serving bowl and pour the sauce over. Toss well and chill before serving.

Crabmeat Pastry

After a long cocktail hour, the dinner guests to whom I served this needed an interesting appetizer. This worked. Crab makes a savory filling for flaky strudle pastry. This is best served hot from the oven, but is quite good reheated. Phyllo is a paper-thin pastry "leaf" that is used for *baklava*, *spanokopita*, and many other Middle Eastern dishes. It can be bought at Greek or Middle Eastern groceries or at specialty shops. It is often sold frozen, wrapped in plastic, and should be defrosted overnight, in its own wrapper, in the refrigerator. Since it becomes brittle and unworkable quickly when exposed to air, you should keep it covered with a layer of waxed paper covered with a very slightly damp cloth as you work, but don't let it get *wet*, or it will stick together.

FILLING

	6	12	20	50
onions, chopped	1	2	4	7
butter	5 tbs	10 tbs	2 sticks	1¼ lbs
all-purpose flour	2 tbs	4 tbs	6 tbs	¾ c
milk, at room temperature	2 c	4 c	6 c	10 c
parsley, chopped	1 tsp	2 tbs	4 tbs	7 tbs
fresh dill, chopped	1 tsp	2 tbs	4 tbs	7 tbs
mushrooms, chopped	½ c	1 c	1¾ c	2½ c
canned pimiento, chopped	1 tbs	2 tbs	4 tbs	7 tbs
eggs, hard-boiled and chopped	2	4	7	14
Tabasco, to taste, or	1 dash	¼ tsp	½ tsp	1 tsp
Worcestershire sauce	1 tbs	2 tbs	3½ tbs	4¾ tbs
sherry	1 tsp	2 tsp	3½ tsp	4¾ tsp
dried basil	1 pinch	½ tsp	¾ tsp	1 tbs
salt and pepper		(to taste)		
crabmeat, fresh, frozen, or canned	1½ lbs	3 lbs	5 lbs	10 lbs
breadcrumbs, very fine	½ c	1 c	1¾ c	4 c

	½ lb	1 lb	1½ lbs	3 lbs
phyllo				
melted butter for phyllo	¾ c	1½ c	2⅔ c	5 c

Pick over the crabmeat carefully for shell and cartilage. Then, in a heavy saucepan, sauté the onion in the butter until golden, then stir in the flour. Add the milk slowly as you cook, stirring, over low heat; continue to stir until thick and smooth. Remove from the heat and add all the remaining ingredients except the phyllo and the melted butter. If the mixture seems loose, add more bread-crumbs; if thick, more milk.

Preheat the oven to 350°.

Prepare 9 × 13 × 1½-inch pan[s] by brushing melted butter on the bottom. [One 9 × 13 × 1½-inch pan will serve six very large portions, two pans, twelve large portions. For twenty, use two 9 × 13 × 1½-inch pans and have leftovers. For fifty, reduce portion size and use three 9 × 13 × 1½-inch pans and one 10-inch square pan, or four of the first size.] Lay one sheet of phyllo at a time in the pan, brushing each with melted butter, until you have about ten layers. Spread the crab-meat mixture over the phyllo, and then lay ten more sheets of phyllo, brushing each with butter, over the crabmeat. Pour the remaining melted butter over the top and bake for 45 minutes, or until golden brown. If you are baking three pans at once, it may take longer. Cut into approximately 3-inch squares to serve.

NOTE: This may be made the day before serving, and reheated for 15 to 20 minutes before cutting.

Momos

Momos are meat-filled dumplings, native to Tibet, which combine the texture and style of Chinese dumplings with a spicy meat filling reminiscent of Indian curries. I learned to make these in Nepal, where we used water buffalo for the ground meat filling, but a mixture of beef and pork seems to work almost as well. These can be made in large quantities and frozen after they have been steamed, for later resteaming or frying in oil. They are traditionally served with a clear broth that is garnished with chopped scallion or a spicy tomato sauce with powdered red pepper to taste.

DOUGH

	6	12	20	50
unbleached, all-purpose flour	2 c	4 c	6½ c	12 c
cold water		(as needed)		

FILLING

	6	12	20	50
ground beef and pork, mixed	1½ lbs	3 lbs	5 lbs	12 lbs
ground coriander	1 tsp	2 tsp	3½ tsp	2½ tbs
ground cumin	1 tsp	2 tsp	3½ tsp	2½ tbs
ground turmeric	1 tsp	2 tsp	3½ tsp	2½ tbs
ground cinnamon	1 tsp	2 tsp	3½ tsp	2½ tbs
coarse salt	1 tsp	2 tsp	3½ tsp	2½ tbs
cayenne	¼ tsp	½ tsp	¾ tsp	2 tsp
mustard * or peanut oil	1 tbs	2 tbs	3¾ tbs	8 tbs
scallion bunches, cleaned and very finely minced, including the green stalk	1	2	4	8

* Mustard oil is a mild vegetable oil available in Indian, Middle Eastern, or specialty markets. Since it is not flavored, peanut oil or any vegetable oil can be substituted.

SAUCE

	6	12	20	50
mustard or corn oil	2 tbs	3 tbs	5 tbs	½ c
small onions, finely chopped	1	2	4	8
dried fenugreek	2 tsp	4 tsp	6 tsp	4 tbs
or				
fenugreek seed	1 tsp	2 tsp	3 tsp	2 tbs
fresh tomatoes	4	8	12	30
cayenne	(to taste)			
fresh coriander leaves	3 tbs	6 tbs	10 tbs	1½ c
or				
ground coriander	1 tsp	2 tsp	3 tsp	2½ tbs
combined with				
fresh parsley	3 tbs	6 tbs	10 tbs	1½ c
salt	(to taste)			

Prepare the dough first. Place the flour in a large bowl. [For the largest amount, prepare the dough in two batches.] Make a well in the middle and pour in a little cold water, stirring the flour in from the sides. Keep adding water until the dough sticks together in a ball and is soft. Place the dough on a tabletop and knead, adding more flour, if necessary, to make a springy, elastic dough. Place in a bowl and cover with a dish towel while you prepare the filling.

If you buy the meat ready ground, if possible have the butcher grind them together again, or you can grind them at home using a fine blade on the meat grinder.

Place the meat in a bowl, then add all the remaining filling ingredients. Mix it well with hands for about 3 minutes, until the mixture is smooth.

To assemble the *momos,* break off a piece of dough the size of a small walnut. Roll it into a ball and then flatten, with fingers or rolling pin, on a floured surface. Be careful not to make the dough in the center too thin; the edges should be thinner than the center. Place a small ball of filling in the center of each round and fold, which you may do in one of the following ways.

The easiest is to fold the dough over the filling, making a half-moon shape, and to pinch the edges shut in a scallop pattern. The traditional way is to make a round dumpling with the edges gathered in pleats at the top, and sealed in the center. To do this—and to avoid having too much dough lumped at the top—place a small ball of filling in the center of the circle of dough. With the circle

flat on one hand, pinch a pleat in the edge of the circle with the thumb and forefinger of the other, and holding the pleat add successive pleats to it with the forefinger, turning until the edges are all gathered in pleats over the filling. Twist the top together.

Place the dumplings on a plate that has been dusted with flour. When they are all done, put them on greased plates in a steamer so that they do not touch each other and steam them for about 25 minutes. They may then be frozen, or cooled and fried in oil. Fried or steamed, they may be piled on a hot platter and eaten accompanied by the following sauce.

SAUCE

Heat the oil in a saucepan and sauté the onion until golden. Add the fenugreek seeds, if used, and sauté, stirring, for 3 minutes. Chop the tomatoes and any fresh herbs you are using. Then, add the tomatoes, fenugreek leaves if used, cayenne, coriander or parsley and coriander, and salt and simmer, partially covered, for 30 minutes. If the sauce dries out, add a little water; it should have the consistency of a light spaghetti sauce (by the way, this is a Tibetan noodle sauce as well). Let cool to room temperature for serving with *momos*.

Salad Méchouia

Far from the ordinary tuna salad, *méchouia* lifts that canned fish out of banality. A rich combination of tuna, peppers, and oil, to be served with Syrian bread as a first course to a Middle Eastern meal, this recipe comes from Morocco and is excellent with a *couscous* dinner.

Syrian bread is a flat, circular loaf that can be split into two layers. A filling may be put inside. Syrian bread (sometimes called *pita*) is available in some supermarkets or in specialty shops.

Harissa is a hot Moroccan pepper paste that is available in tins. It is sold in specialty shops. For a substitute use Tabasco sauce and mashed hot chili peppers.

	6	12	20	50
green peppers	2	4	8	20
large tomatoes	2	4	8	20
capers	1 tbs	2 tbs	4 tbs	10 tbs
olive oil	¼ c	½ c	1 c	2½ c
juice of fresh lemons	½	1	2	5
or				
bottled lemon juice to taste, or	1 tbs	2 tbs	4 tbs	1 c
tuna, 7-ounce cans, flaked	1	2	4	8–10
garlic cloves, finely minced	2	4	6	14
salt	(to taste)			
freshly ground pepper	(to taste)			
Harissa	(to taste)			

Toast the peppers and tomatoes together over charcoal (this can be messy, so surround the area with foil) or char them on a gas flame. Or place under broiler (again on foil) for 20 minutes, turning occasionally, until cooked and well charred. Let cool for a few minutes, then peel the peppers and tomatoes with your fingers and place all the pulp in a bowl.

Add the remaining ingredients, tasting for balance of hot and salt and acid, and cool to room temperature before serving.

NOTE: This does not need refrigeration but should be kept in a cool place overnight. It can be stored in the refrigerator but should be brought back to room temperature before serving. It is traditionally very hot and very oily.

Moroccan Chermoulah

This is another spicy Moroccan appetizer, which should be salty to "increase appetite." It is a rich, peppery, and oily accompaniment for Syrian bread.

	6	12	20	50
large green peppers, seeded and cut into thin strips	2	4	8	20
whole garlic cloves, peeled	4–5	8–10	16–20	36–40
salt	¼ tsp	½ tsp	1 tsp	2½ tsp
paprika	¼ tsp	½ tsp	1 tsp	2½ tsp
olive oil	1 c	2 c	3½ c	5 c
wine vinegar	¼ c	½ c	¾ c	1½ c
ground coriander	2 pinches	½ tsp	1 tsp	2 tsp

Put all the ingredients into a saucepan and cook slowly for about 20 minutes, or until the peppers are tender. Spoon into a clean jar and refrigerate. Before serving, bring to room temperature and remove the garlic cloves.

NOTE: This does not *need* refrigeration, but should be kept in a cool place. It can be made several days ahead.

Homous

A Middle-Eastern chick-pea appetizer, served with Syrian bread, this is popular in Israel and throughout the Middle East, and is becoming a cocktail party stand-by in the United States.

In this recipe, it is important to keep tasting and adding things—some people like more garlic, some less lemon juice, some like it oily.

Sesame paste is also known as *tahini*, and can be bought in cans or jars in Middle Eastern stores and specialty shops. It is ground from sesame seeds, and is used in pastries and savories. It should be stirred well before using, as the oil often separates.

	6	12	20	50
20-oz cans cooked chick-peas, drained and rinsed	1	2	3½	8
sesame paste	½ c	1 c	1¾ c	4 c
fresh lemon juice, to taste, or	½–¾ c	1–1½ c	2–3 c	3–4 c
garlic cloves	2	4	8	12
salt	1 tsp	2 tsp	1½ tbs	3 tbs
olive oil, if necessary				
Italian parsley, for garnish				

Place all the ingredients except the olive oil and parsley in a blender (in batches) and blend until smooth. Repeat until all are used up. Add water to make a loose paste, and add a little olive oil, if necessary, to loosen it. Refrigerate (it will keep overnight), then bring to room temperature to serve. Stir before serving on a flat plate, garnished with the parsley.

Baba G'hanouj

The reader may have begun to detect a bias toward Middle Eastern appetizers. This eggplant "paste" is addictive. No matter how much you make, it will all be eaten.

Sesame paste is also known as *tahini*, and can be bought in cans or jars in Middle Eastern stores and specialty shops. It is ground from sesame seeds, and is used in pastries and savories. It should be stirred well before using, as the oil often separates.

	6	12	20	50
large eggplants	2	4	7	15
juice of whole lemons, to taste, or	2	4	7	15 or 1½ c
sesame paste	2 tbs	4 tbs	7 tbs	15 tbs
salt		(to taste)		
large garlic clove[s]	1	2	4	10
olive oil to taste, or	2 tbs	4 tbs	7 tbs	15 tbs
fresh parsley, chopped	¼ c	½ c	¾ c	2 c

Cook the eggplant over a gas flame or charcoal, or under the broiler of an electric stove, until charred all over, 30 minutes or more. If cooking a large number, char first, then place in a 325° oven on baking sheets until the insides are completely soft. Set them aside to cool for about 1 hour.

Peel and discard the burnt skin, then put the flesh into a mixing bowl and immediately add the lemon juice. Mash very well, then add the tahini and blend well. Add the salt; mash the garlic and add. Stir well and chill. Serve in a flat dish, with olive oil poured over. Garnish with the chopped parsley and serve with Syrian bread.

Dolmathis

Ellen Butterfield taught me to roll these—the first of my Middle Eastern recipes.

Grape leaves, stuffed with herbed rice and braised, make an excellent appetizer. If obtainable, use fresh grapevine leaves, young and unsprayed. Prepare them by washing and placing them in layers with coarse salt. Pour boiling water over them and let stand for 1 hour.

	6	12	20	50
small onions, finely chopped	1	2	3	8
butter or olive oil	¼ c	½ c	¾ c	2 c
granulated sugar	1 tbs	2 tbs	3 tbs	8 tbs
salt	1 tbs	2 tbs	3 tbs	8 tbs
freshly ground black pepper	1 tbs	2 tbs	3 tbs	8 tbs
raw rice	1 c	2 c	3½ c	8 c
fresh parsley	2 tbs	4 tbs	7 tbs	¾ c
and				
fresh dill, finely chopped	2 tbs	4 tbs	7 tbs	¾ c
or				
fresh mint, finely chopped	4 tbs	8 tbs	12 tbs	1½ c
fresh lemon juice	1 lemon	2 lemons	3 lemons	1 c
fresh grape leaves	36	72	126	216
or				
1-lb jars grape leaves	1	2	3½	6
chicken broth	2 c	4 c	7 c	14 c
olive oil		(to taste)		

GARNISH

lemon wedges				
Greek olives	½ lb	1 lb	1½ lbs	3¼ lbs

Brown the chopped onion very slowly in the butter or oil. Add the sugar, salt, and pepper, then remove from the flame. Fold in the rice, dill, and parsley and stir in the lemon juice.

Drain the leaves (fresh or preserved) and rinse in cold water. To roll the leaves, spread out a leaf with the shiny side down. Place a teaspoon of filling in the center, fold over the sides, then roll up. Place the rolled leaves, with overlapping edges down, in a saucepan, tight against each other. You may put them in layers.

Pour the broth slowly over the rolls. Simmer very gently for 45 minutes, adding more broth if necessary; check every 15 minutes. Let cool in the hot broth, then drain.

Arrange the grape leaves on a platter and sprinkle with olive oil. Serve at room temperature, garnished with lemon wedges and Greek olives.

NOTE: These can be kept in a cool place instead of the refrigerator.

Quiches

I like serving individual quiches for the first course of an elaborate dinner. They are rather filling, so make them small —I use small foil pans, about 3 inches across. Or make several large quiches to slice. If you make a large quantity of the basic egg and cream filling, you can make several kinds of quiches for a buffet, in one baking, simply by adding cooked spinach to some, grated cheese and sautéed onion to others, and raw shrimp to still others. (Or cooked artichoke hearts, or blanched asparagus tips, or use your imagination.)

Use any standard recipe for pie crust, chilled for at least two hours before you roll it out. If making more than one pie (serving six) it is better to make it fresh in separate batches, rather than mixing one large bowl for twelve, twenty, or fifty. I find it is easier to control the mixing of the flour and fat this way.

One standard 9-inch quiche serves six. One batch of pastry for a 9-inch quiche will make about 4 small tart-sized quiches.

BASIC QUICHE MIXTURE

	6	12	20	50
eggs	4	8	16	34
salt	½ tsp	1 tsp	2 tsp	1 tbs
cayenne		(to taste)		
grated nutmeg		(to taste)		
light cream	1 pt	2 pts	4 pts	8 pts

GARNISH SUGGESTIONS

	6	12	20	50
raw shrimp, shelled, deveined, and chopped	1 c	2 c	4 c	2 lbs
Swiss cheese, grated	½ lb	1 lb	2 lbs	4 lbs
onion, finely chopped sautéed in	½ c	1 c	2 c	4 c
butter, until brown	1 tbs	4 tbs	4 tbs	½ lb
10-oz packages fresh spinach, cleaned, chopped, and cooked in the water clinging to the leaves	1	2	4	8

Preheat the oven to 375°.

Combine all the ingredients for the basic quiche mixture and beat lightly, then set aside while you roll out the pie crust to fit the pans. Add one or more of the garnishes above and pour in the basic quiche mixture, to about ¼ inch of the top of the crust. Bake for about 40 minutes (the small pans will take less time).

NOTE: These can be served warm or cool, but they are best tepid, I think.

Phyllis Blumberg's Chopped Chicken Livers

Chopped chicken livers make a classic appetizer. Add a few drops of Cognac and it will be unforgettable. It's better if it's made the day before.

	6	12	20	50
chicken fat	4 tbs	8 tbs	¾ c	1 lb
or				
butter	½ stick	1 stick	1½ sticks	1 lb
raw chicken livers	1½ lbs	3 lbs	5 lbs	10 lbs
eggs, hard-boiled	2	4	7	12
medium onions	2	4	7	16
salt		(to taste)		
freshly ground black pepper		(to taste)		
Cognac (optional)	1 tbs	2 tbs	3½ tbs	7 tbs

SERVING

pumpernickel bread, sliced
onions, sliced in rings

Melt the fat or butter in a skillet and sauté the chicken livers, in batches, until firm. Remove from the heat and let stand while peeling the eggs and cutting the onions into quarters. Reserve the melted fat or butter in the pan.

Using a meat grinder, grind the livers, eggs, and onions together. Add the reserved melted fat or butter and salt, pepper, and Cognac to taste. Mound the mixture in a large serving dish and chill overnight. Serve with wedges of pumpernickel (see recipe on page 21) and onions sliced in rings.

Pumpernickel Bread

Pumpernickel is a bread with a secret. Some say it is prunes that distinguish it; this recipe claims it is chocolate. It will make three round loaves, which, thinly sliced, should provide appetizer portions (with chopped chicken livers, for instance) for fifty.

DOUGH

unsweetened chocolate squares (1 oz each)	2
yellow cornmeal	¾ c
cold mashed potatoes	2 c
warm water, 115°	3½ c
molasses	¼ c
salt	2 tbs
butter or margarine	1 tbs
caraway seeds	2 tsp
active-dry-yeast packages	2
rye flour	3 c
all-purpose flour	8 c

GLAZE

egg yolk	1
water	3 tbs

Melt the chocolate in a double boiler over simmering water. Then, in a large bowl, combine the cornmeal, potatoes, 3 cups of the warm water, chocolate, molasses, salt, butter or margarine, and caraway seeds.

In a very large bowl (I use a 5-gallon kettle) place the remaining ½ cup of warm water and sprinkle on the yeast, then stir to dissolve.

Stir in the cornmeal mixture and rye flour and beat hard until well mixed. Stir in 3 cups of the all-purpose flour to make a soft dough.

Turn onto a floured board or tabletop and knead in additional flour, to 5 or more cups, to make a smooth, elastic dough. This will take about 10 minutes.

Place the dough in a greased bowl—or wash out the kettle and dry and grease it—then turn the dough to grease the top, cover, and let rise in a warm, draft-free place for about 1 hour, or until doubled in bulk. Punch down, then let rise again for 30 minutes.

Punch the dough down and turn onto a lightly floured board or table. Divide into three equal parts, shape into round loaves, and place on greased baking sheets. Cover with tea towels and let rise until double—about 45 minutes. Meanwhile, preheat the oven to 350°.

Mix the water and egg yolk for glaze and brush the loaves with the egg-yolk liquid. Bake loaves for 1 hour, or until tapping on the bottom of the loaves produces a hollow sound. Cool thoroughly on racks, then wrap well and refrigerate. This recipe makes 3 round loaves.

NOTE: This bread slices best when one day old. It can also be successfully frozen.

Pâté de Campagne

Coarse pâtés of this type are excellent for informal parties or picnics. You can substitute other meats, such as veal, or other meat livers, for those suggested.

	6	12	20	50
small onions	2	4	7	17
butter	2 tbs	4 tbs	7 tbs	2 sticks
fresh, boneless pork	½ lb	1 lb	1¾ lbs	4 lbs
raw dark chicken meat, boneless	½ lb	1 lb	1¾ lbs	4 lbs
chicken or pork liver	½ lb	1 lb	1¾ lbs	4 lbs
eggs	1	2	3	7
Cognac, port, or sherry	2 tbs	4 tbs	7 tbs	⅔ c
garlic cloves, finely minced	2	4	7	15
freshly ground black pepper	½ tsp	1 tsp	1¾ tsp	4 tsp
allspice		(to taste)		
thyme	½ tsp	1 tsp	1¾ tsp	4 tsp
bay leaves, crumbled	1	2	3	6
salt		(to taste)		
pork fat	½ lb	1 lb	1¾ lbs	4 lbs

Preheat the oven to 350°.

Sauté the minced onion in the butter until soft, but not browned. Put the pork, chicken, and liver through a meat grinder twice. Beat in all the other ingredients except the pork fat, then sauté a small spoonful of the mixture and taste. Correct the seasoning.

Slice the fat into very thin sheets and use it to line a 9 × 4 × 3-inch loaf pan or terrine [two, four, or eight 9 × 4 × 3-inch loaf pans]. Put the pâté mixture into the lined pan[s], then put the pans in roasting pan[s] and surround them with hot water at least halfway up their sides. Cover the pan[s] with foil and bake in the roaster[s] for 1½ hours or until the juices from the pâté run clear and yellow, not pink or red.

Remove the pan[s] from oven and pour the water out of the roaster[s]. Replace the loaf pan[s] in the roaster pan[s] and place a small dish or board on the pâté, with a 1-pound weight or equivalent (such as a heavy can), to press and firm up the pâté as it cools to room temperature. Remove the weight and refrigerate.

NOTE: The pâté is best eaten 2 days after it is made.

in oven

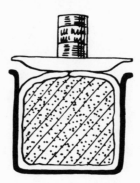

in refrigerator

Swedish Limpa Bread

This is a sweet, rich rye bread that goes well with unsalted butter. It is good with a thick-soup and salad meal.

DOUGH

	2 loaves	4 loaves	8 loaves
warm water	2 c	4 c	8 c
shortening	2 tbs	4 tbs	8 tbs
aniseed, crushed	1 tsp	2 tsp	4 tsp
or			
fennel seeds, crushed	1 tsp	2 tsp	4 tsp
molasses	¼ c	½ c	1 c
light-brown sugar	⅓ c	⅔ c	1⅓ c
active-dry-yeast packages	1	2	4
all-purpose flour	3½ c	7 c	14 c
salt	1 tbs	2 tbs	4 tbs
rye flour	2¼ c	4½ c	9 c
vegetable oil	1 tsp	2 tsp	4 tsp

GLAZE

egg yolk	1	2	3
water	1 tbs	2 tbs	3 tbs

Combine 1¼ cups [2½ cups, 5 cups] of the water, the shortening, aniseed, molasses, and brown sugar in a saucepan and bring to a boil. Boil for 3 minutes, then cool to lukewarm (about 45 minutes).

In a large bowl, dissolve the yeast in the remaining ¾ cups [1½ cups, 3 cups] warm water. Add the molasses mixture and the all-purpose flour and beat until smooth. Cover this sponge and let it rise until doubled in bulk (1½ to 2 hours).

Stir down the sponge and add the salt and rye flour. Brush the surface with oil, cover, and let rise again until doubled in bulk. Meanwhile, preheat the oven to 350°.

Punch the dough down and knead it for 8 to 10 minutes. Form the dough into 2 [4, 8] smooth, round balls and place on greased baking sheets. Brush the top of the loaves with the egg yolk and water (mixed together) and bake at 350° for 50 minutes, or until hollow sounding when rapped with the knuckles. Remove from the baking sheets and cool on cake racks. The texture is best after the bread has thoroughly cooled.

NOTE: This bread can be frozen.

Cream of Mushroom Soup

Mushrooms make a fine and luxurious soup. To make this soup even more elegant, stir in a few tablespoons of sherry at the very end.

	6	12	20	50
onion, minced	¼ c	½ c	1 c	2½ c
butter	5 tbs	10 tbs	2 sticks	5 sticks
all-purpose flour	3 tbs	6 tbs	10 tbs	⅔ c
boiling chicken stock	6 c	12 c	5 qts	12 qts
or				
boiling canned chicken broth	6 c	12 c	5 qts	12 qts
mushrooms	1 lb	2 lbs	3½ lbs	6 lbs
small bay leaves	1	2	4	8
thyme	pinch	½ tsp	1 tsp	2½ tsp
salt	2 pinches	½ tsp	¾ tsp	1 tsp
lemon juice	1 tsp	2 tsp	1½ tbs	3 tbs
heavy cream	½ c	1 c	1½ c	3 c

GARNISH

fresh parsley, chopped	2 tbs	3½ tbs	½ c	1¼ c

Clean the mushrooms carefully. Separate the stems from the caps and then chop them both. Keep the chopped stems separate from the chopped caps.

Cook the onion slowly in 3 tablespoons [6 tablespoons, 10 tablespoons, 3 sticks] of the butter till tender but not browned. Add the flour and stir over low heat for 5 minutes without browning. Remove the pot from the heat and beat in the hot chicken stock or broth. Season to taste, then stir in the chopped mushroom stems and simmer with the bay leaves and thyme for 20 minutes or more. Strain, pressing the juices out of mushrooms. Discard the mushroom stems and return the soup to the kettle.

Melt the remaining butter in a separate saucepan, and add the mushroom caps, salt, and lemon juice. Cover and cook slowly for 5 minutes. Add the mushrooms and pan juices to the soup and simmer for 10 minutes. Before serving, add the cream while beating with a wire whip. Heat slowly but *do not let boil*. Garnish each bowl with parsley and serve.

NOTE: This can be refrigerated and served the next day.

Cold Cucumber Soup

Cucumbers are great in soup as well as in salad. Though this soup is served cold, don't hesitate to serve it with a heavy winter meal. Your guests will be delighted.

	6	12	20	50
peeled cucumber, coarsely chopped	3 c	6 c	10 c	15 large
chicken broth	1½ c	3 c	5 c	12 c
light cream	1½ c	3 c	5 c	12 c
chives, chopped	⅓ c	⅔ c	1⅓ c	2⅔ c
celery leaves, chopped	⅓ c	⅔ c	1⅓ c	2⅔ c
fresh parsley, chopped	4 sprigs	⅓ c	⅔ c	2 c
all-purpose flour	3 tbs	6 tbs	10 tbs	⅔ c
salt	(to taste)			
freshly ground black pepper	(to taste)			

GARNISH

lemon rind, grated	1 lemon	2 lemons	3 lemons	7 lemons
	or	or	or	or
	1 tbs	2 tbs	3 tbs	7 tbs

Combine all the soup ingredients except the salt and pepper and blend in small batches in a blender until smooth. Transfer to a saucepan as blended and heat, stirring, until the soup is very hot, slightly thickened, and has lost any floury taste. Add salt and pepper to taste. Cool, then refrigerate.

Before serving, stir thoroughly and garnish each bowl with a little grated lemon rind.

NOTE: This can be made the day before serving.

Cucumber-Yogurt Soup

This soup is similar to the cucumber *raita* on page 135. It is excellent as a starter for any summer meal.

	6	12	20	50
medium cucumbers	2	4	7	15
salt		(to taste)		
chicken broth	3 c	6 c	3 qts	6 qts
plain yogurt	2 c	4 c	7 c	8 pts
freshly ground black pepper		(to taste)		

GARNISH

scallions (including the green), finely chopped	3	6	10	25

Peel the cucumbers with a vegetable peeler. Slice in half lengthwise and scoop out the seeds with a teaspoon. Chop half of the cucumbers roughly, setting the rest aside, and sprinkle with salt. Place in a colander and let drain onto a plate for about 30 minutes. Rinse and dry on paper towels.

Puree the chopped cucumber in a blender with a small amount of the chicken broth. (You will have to do this in small batches.) Put the blended cucumber and all the remaining chicken broth into a large bowl or kettle. Grate the rest of the cucumber into shreds and add.

Put the yogurt into a large bowl or kettle and add the cucumber mixture slowly, stirring well. Season to taste. Garnish with finely chopped scallion and serve.

Broccoli Soup

Broccoli seems an unlikely soup vegetable, but this is one of the most delicate and delicious soups I know. On no account forget the sesame seeds.

	6	12	20	50
fresh broccoli bunches	1	2	4	8
chicken stock	5 c	10 c	5 qts	10 qts
or				
canned broth	5 c	10 c	5 qts	10 qts
heavy cream	1 c	2 c	4 c	8 c
salt		(to taste)		
freshly ground black pepper		(to taste)		

GARNISH

	6	12	20	50
butter	2 tbs	4 tbs	7 tbs	2 sticks
sesame seeds	2 tbs	4 tbs	7 tbs	¾ c

Carefully peel the stems of the broccoli, then cut the whole bunches into small chunks. Bring the broth to a boil, add the broccoli, and cook it until it falls apart. Puree the soup in a blender or put it through a food mill, and let cool. Add the heavy cream.

Set the soup aside if it is not to be served immediately, and refrigerate when cool. When ready to serve, reheat, being careful not to boil the soup, and add salt and pepper to taste.

In a separate saucepan, melt the butter and add the sesame seeds. Cook over medium heat, stirring, until the seeds just begin to brown. Don't let them burn. Add the butter and sesame seeds to the soup just before serving.

Garlic Soup

Garlic soup can be a light first course or a thick main dish. Despite what seems to be an extraordinary amount of garlic, it loses its "fire" and takes on a lovely, nutty taste in the cooking.

Garlic cloves are easier to peel if they are first dropped in boiling water for about 10 seconds and then drained in a colander.

	6	12	20	50
garlic cloves, peeled	1 c	2 c	3½ c	7 c
small onions, chopped	1	2	3	8
olive oil	6 tbs	¾ c	1 c and 7 tbs	2¾ c
canned Italian plum tomatoes, drained	⅔ c	1⅓ c	2 c	6 c
chicken or beef stock	1 qt	2 qts	4 qts	8 qts
salt		(to taste)		
freshly ground black pepper		(to taste)		
thyme	½ tsp	1 tsp	2 tsp	5 tsp
bay leaves	1	2	3	6
egg yolks	1	2	3	7

GARNISH

	6	12	20	50
fresh parsley, chopped	¼ c	½ c	1 c	2 c
Romano cheese, grated	1 c	1½ c	2 c	4½ c

Mince the garlic, then place it, along with the onion and 2 tablespoons [4 tablespoons, 7 tablespoons, 3¼ cups] of the oil, in a deep saucepan. Heat slowly and cook, stirring, until soft. Do not brown. Add the tomatoes, stock, salt, pepper, thyme, and bay leaves and simmer for 40 minutes. Press through a sieve or food mill and set aside in a cool place until ready to serve.

Just before serving, place the egg yolk[s] in a small bowl and beat well. Drop by drop add the remaining olive oil to the yolks, as if for a mayonnaise, beating constantly until thick. Bring the soup just to a boil and add, little by little, the hot soup to the mayonnaise, beating constantly. After a cup of soup has been added, you may safely pour the egg-soup mixture back into the pot, but do not allow it to boil. Garnish with the parsley and serve with French bread and grated Romano cheese in a separate bowl.

NOTE: This soup may be made heartier by adding potatoes, more tomatoes, or other soup vegetables after straining. Cook until tender, and continue as above. You might even add some garlic sausages, cut in chunks. Serve with salad and bread as a main luncheon dish.

Spinach Soup

A simple but rich-tasting soup. You can substitute margarine for the sautéing butter, and eliminate the rest, if you like.

	6	12	20	50
fresh spinach	½ lb	1 lb	1¾ lbs	3½ lbs
butter	6 tbs	1 stick and 4 tbs	2 sticks and 5 tbs	4 sticks and 6 tbs
onion, chopped	1 c	2 c	3½ c	7 c
medium potatoes, peeled and quartered	4	8	14	28
chicken stock	2 c	4 c	7 c	3 qts
water	2 c	4 c	7 c	3 qts
salt		(to taste)		
freshly ground black pepper		(to taste)		
heavy cream	1 c	2 c	3½ c	3 pts

Rinse the spinach well, and shred with a large sharp knife. Heat 4 tablespoons [1 stick, 1¾ stick, 3 sticks] of the butter in a large saucepan and cook the onion until wilted. Add the spinach, potatoes, stock, and water and cook until the potatoes are tender (about 25 minutes).

Put the soup through a food mill or sieve (not a blender!). Season with salt and pepper and stir in the cream. Bring just to a boil and stir in the remaining butter if desired. Serve at once.

NOTE: If made ahead, do not add the cream and remaining butter until just before serving time.

New England Clam Chowder

This chowder is everything it should be: fresh-tasting, rich (a main dish), and *authentic*. The most important things to remember are: keep the sand out, use salt pork, and serve it the day after it is made. I will not dispute the claims of Manhattan chowder to "authenticity," but I will defend *this* chowder's superior delectability.

	6	12	20	50
steamer clams, scrubbed and picked over	3 lbs	6 lbs	10 lbs	20 lbs
salt pork, rind removed	½ lb	½ lb	⅞ lb	2 lbs
medium onions	1	2	4	8
milk	4 c	8 c	2 qts	4 qts
salt		(to taste)		
freshly ground black pepper		(to taste)		
medium potatoes	3	6	10	24

Place the clams in a large kettle with about 2 inches of water. [For twenty, steam two batches; for fifty, four batches.] Turn the heat to high, cover the pot, and cook until the clams open wide. Set aside to cool until you can handle them. Reserve the cooking liquid.

Remove the clams from their shells, washing them in the reserved cooking liquid to remove extra sand. Pour off the liquid, leaving the sand in the bottom of your pot. Peel each "neck" and chop off, then chop all the necks together and set aside. Place the stomachs in a bowl.

Chop salt pork very finely. Put it in a large, heavy saucepan and heat slowly until it has rendered its fat and the pieces are golden. Remove the pieces and drain on paper towels. Peel the potatoes and dice them. Add the onion to the rendered fat and cook over medium heat until golden. Add the clam necks and simmer 3 minutes, then add the clam stomachs, potatoes, and reserved clam steaming liquid. (You must be careful not to include any sand; if you are in doubt, strain it through several layers of cheesecloth.) Simmer until the potatoes are *just* tender, about 15 minutes.

Add the milk and salt and pepper to taste, and heat. After the milk has been added, do not let the chowder boil. Add the browned salt pork bits. Let cool before refrigerating, to serve the next day.

Cauliflower Soup

Cauliflower is not a versatile vegetable, perhaps because of its powerful savor. This soup is rich and delicate, and will be loved by the staunchest cauliflower hater.

	6	12	20	50
butter	3 tbs	6 tbs	10 tbs	1½ c
medium onions	2	4	7	15
chicken broth	4 c	8 c	14 c	8 qts
heads of cauliflower	1	2	4	8
light cream	½ pt	1 pt	1½ pts	3½ pts
		(or as needed)		
salt		(to taste)		
freshly ground black pepper		(to taste)		

GARNISH

fresh parsley
   or
fresh dill
   or
fresh coriander, finely chopped
	2 tbs	4 tbs	6 tbs	1 c

Melt the butter in a large, heavy saucepan and cook the onion in it over low heat until golden. Add the chicken broth and bring to a boil.

Wash and drain the cauliflower; then separate it into florets. Add the cauliflower to the broth and reduce the heat to a simmer. Let cook until cauliflower is tender.

Puree the broth and cauliflower in a food mill. Add cream to thin, and salt and pepper to taste. Garnish with the chopped fresh herbs.

NOTE: This can be served cold.

Fermented Watercress Soup

Do not be put off by the bizarre sound of this soup: it is quite interesting and delicious. It is a potato-based soup, made on the pattern of a vichyssoise, and with the interesting addition of "aged" cress. My thanks to Mr. Shi, who first had this soup in 1918 in Chicago, and remembers it vividly now.

Dried watercress is available in Chinese markets.

	6	12	20	50
fresh watercress bunches	3	6	10	20
or				
dried watercress	1 oz	2 ozs	3½ ozs	7 ozs
salt, to taste, or	1 tbs	2 tbs	3½ tbs	¾ c
small onion, chopped	1	2	3	8
leeks, cleaned and chopped	2	4	7	15
butter	3 tbs	6 tbs	10 tbs	1 c
medium potatoes	4	8	15	30
chicken broth		(as needed)		
freshly ground black pepper		(to taste)		

Place the watercress (fresh or dried), washed, cleaned, and dried, in a glass or enameled bowl. Add salt and cover with cold water. Set in the refrigerator for 3 days. Drain and chop.

Place the chopped onions and leeks in a heavy saucepan with the butter and sauté gently until translucent and golden. Peel and quarter the potatoes and add them to the onions and leeks. Cover with chicken broth. Simmer gently until the potatoes are cooked through (about 25 minutes).

Drain and chop the watercress and add to the soup. Puree in a blender or put through a food mill, then thin with more chicken broth until smoothly soupy. Season to taste and serve.

Lentil Soup with Mettwurst

A rich and filling soup, with which you will need only bread, salad, and dessert to make a good lunch or supper. Try it with other sausages or cooking salamis, too. Any uncooked (but smoked) fine-grained sausage may be substituted.

	6	12	20	50
dried green lentils	1 c	2 c	3½ c	7 c
butter	2 tbs	4 tbs	7 tbs	2 sticks
large onion, finely chopped	1	2	3½	8
celery stalks, finely chopped	1	2	3	8
carrots, peeled and thinly sliced	2	4	7	14
bay leaves	1	2	3	5
thyme	pinch	½ tsp	1 tsp	2½ tsp
bouillon	1 qt	2 qts	3½ qts	7 qts
or				
rich chicken stock	1 qt	2 qts	3½ qts	7 qts
mettwurst	½ lb	1 lb	2 lbs	4 lbs
salt		(to taste)		
freshly ground black pepper		(to taste)		

Soak the lentils in water to cover overnight.

The next day, drain the lentils well. Melt the butter in a large saucepan and add the chopped onion, celery, and carrots, then the bay leaves and thyme. Let simmer, covered, for about 15 minutes. Add the bouillon or stock, lentils, and sausage and cook at a gentle simmer for about 2 hours, or until the lentils are tender.

Remove the sausage and set aside. Put the soup in a blender in small batches and blend until smooth. Leave about one-quarter of the soup unblended and add to the smooth soup for "texture."

Slice the reserved sausage and add to the soup with salt and pepper to taste.

NOTE: The soup can be reheated, but more stock or water will be needed because lentils thicken as they stand. It can also be kept in a cool place, unrefrigerated.

Senegalese Soup

Senegalese soup is a smooth cream of chicken with curry. A classic French adaptation of Oriental tastes, this soup is elegant and smooth, and acceptable as a beginning to any meal.

	6	12	20	50
onions, chopped	2	4	7	15
celery stalks, chopped	2	4	6	10
apples, peeled and chopped	2	4	7	10
butter	3 tbs	6 tbs	10 tbs	3 sticks
curry powder	2 tbs	4 tbs	8 tbs	¾ c
all-purpose flour	¼ c	½ c	¾ c	2 c
chicken stock or broth	4 c	8 c	4 qts	8 qts
salt		(to taste)		
chili powder		(to taste)		
cayenne		(to taste)		
heavy cream	2 c	4 c	5½ c	10 c

GARNISH

fresh parsley, chopped
   or
avocado, peeled and chopped

In a large saucepan (or two kettles) sauté the onions, celery, and apples in the butter until the mixture is soft but not browned. Add the curry powder and sauté for 2 minutes more, then add the flour, stirring well. Cook, stirring, for a minute or so more. Gradually stir in the chicken stock or broth and cook the soup until it thickens. Add the salt, chili powder, and cayenne to taste.

Puree the mixture in a blender or put through a food mill, a few cups at a time, until smooth. Chill the soup, if serving it cold. Just before serving, stir in the cream and garnish each portion with parsley (hot) or avocado (cold).

NOTE: While the soup can be served hot or cold, it is best (and easiest for a crowd) if served cold.

MAIN DISHES

Spanokopita

This Greek spinach pie is an excellent luncheon dish and can be served lukewarm at a picnic.

Phyllo is a paper-thin pastry "leaf" that is used for *baklava*, *spanokopita*, and many other Middle Eastern dishes. It can be bought at Greek or Middle Eastern groceries or at specialty shops. It is often sold frozen, wrapped in plastic, and should be defrosted overnight, in its own wrapper, in the refrigerator. Since it becomes brittle and unworkable quickly when exposed to air, you should keep it covered with a layer of waxed paper covered with a very slightly damp cloth as you work, but don't let it get *wet*, or it will stick together.

	6	12	20	50
spinach, fresh	2 lbs	4 lbs	7 lbs	15 lbs
scallion bunches	1	2	3	7
olive oil	1 tbs	2 tbs	3½ tbs	8 tbs
feta cheese	1 lb	2 lbs	3½ lbs	7 lbs
or				
feta	½ lb	1 lb	1¾ lbs	3½ lbs
and				
farmer's cheese	½ lb	1 lb	1¾ lbs	3½ lbs
eggs, lightly beaten	7	14	20	30
baking powder	½ tsp	1 tsp	1¾ tsp	3 tsp
salt		(to taste)		
freshly ground black pepper		(to taste)		
phyllo pastry	½ lb	1 lb	1½ lbs	3 lbs
melted butter	½ c	1 c	1½ c	2½ c

Wash, drain, and chop the spinach. (If you are making a large amount, the easiest way is to wash the spinach and cook it in a large kettle, briefly, in the liquid clinging to its leaves, until it wilts. Then chop it.) Chop the scallions, and brown them slightly in a skillet in a little olive oil. Combine the scallions, cheeses, eggs, baking powder, salt, and pepper, and toss with the spinach.

Lay five or six sheets of phyllo, brushing each with butter, into a 9 × 13 × 1½-inch or larger baking pan. Add spinach mixture and cover with 5 or 6 more sheets of phyllo, brushing each with butter. (You can use more phyllo if you like, and spread the spinach between several of the middle layers.) Be sure the top layer of phyllo is an unbroken one. Pour the remaining melted butter over all and bake in a 350° oven until golden. For one pan, this will take about an hour. Serve hot, cut into squares.

Putney School Borscht

This is a Ukrainian borscht, which the Putney School serves at its Harvest Festival. It is a superb winter food, and excellent for crowds because it can be expanded (with the "stretching ingredients") in the last half hour of cooking or reheating. Make it the day before, and keep it chilled until you reheat it. Serve with dark pumpernickel or herb bread, salad, and fruit.

BASIC SOUP

	6	12	20	50
lean stewing beef (rump or chuck)	1 lb	2 lbs	4 lbs	10 lbs
beef or chicken stock	6 c	12 c	6 qts	10 qts
onions, chopped	1 lb	2 lbs	4 lbs	10 lbs
celery stalks, chopped	2	4	7	15
carrots, coarsely chopped	2	4	7	15
canned tomatoes, chopped	1½ c	3 c	7 c	10 c
salt		(to taste)		
freshly ground black pepper		(to taste)		
garlic cloves, finely chopped	1	2	3	6
fresh beet bunches, with greens	1	2	4	8
vinegar or lemon juice	2½ tbs	5 tbs	7 tbs	12 tbs
granulated sugar		(to taste)		
fresh parsley, finely chopped	2 tbs	4 tbs	6 tbs	⅔ c

STRETCHING INGREDIENTS

	5	10	14	20
medium potatoes, peeled and cubed	5	10	14	20
cabbage heads, shredded	½	1	1½	3
		(or as needed)		

	6	12	20	50
hard-boiled eggs	2	4	7	15
cucumbers, peeled and cubed	1	2	3	5
green peppers, chopped	2	4	7	10
radish bunches, sliced	1	2	3	8
sour cream	1 c	1 pt	2 pts	4 pts
celery leaves, chopped				

Cube the meat, place it in the stock, bring to a boil, and skim. Reduce the heat, then add the onions, celery (reserve the leaves for garnish), carrots, tomatoes, salt, pepper, and garlic and let simmer, half-covered.

Cut the stems and leaves off the beets, wash thoroughly, and store in the refrigerator. With a stiff brush, scrub the beet roots under running water. Place in a saucepan full of boiling water and cook until tender. Drain, but save the water. Let the beets cool until you can handle them, then peel and shred on a grater. Set aside.

Clean the beet greens again, removing wilted leaves. Chop the greens, put them in a plastic bag, and store again; the greens should be kept as crisp as possible during the whole process.

When the beef is almost tender (about 1½–2 hours), add the potatoes and cook for 15 minutes more. Add the cabbage, the shredded beet root, lemon or vinegar, and sugar. Cook for 10 minutes longer. Just before serving, add the beet greens and parsley and cook another 10 minutes. Set out the garnishes on a tray and let each guest add to the borscht as desired.

NOTE: This soup can be kept unrefrigerated, in a cool place.

Shrimp with Feta Cheese

Shrimp, like chicken, are good adapters. I particularly like the combination of fresh, slightly acid Greek feta cheese with herb-flavored shrimp. This Mediterranean dish is best prepared with fresh dill and tomatoes, but is excellent in any version.

	6	12	20	50
olive oil	¼ c	½ c	13 tbs	¾ c
onions, finely chopped	½ c	1 c	1½ c	4 c
garlic cloves, finely chopped	2	4	6	10
parsley, finely chopped	½ c	1 c	1¾ c	3 c
fresh dill weed	1 tbs	2 tbs	3½ tbs	½ c
or				
dried dill weed	2 tsp	4 tsp	7 tsp	4 tbs
dry mustard	¼ tsp	½ tsp	1 tsp	1 tbs
granulated sugar	½ tsp	1 tsp	1¾ tsp	1 tbs
tomatoes, fresh	3 c	6 c	3½ lbs	7½ lbs
or				
28-oz cans	1	2	3½	7
tomato sauce	¾ c	1½ c	3 c	6 c
raw shrimp, shelled and deveined	1½ lbs	3 lbs	5½ lbs	12 lbs
feta cheese, crumbled	¾ lb	1½ lbs	3 lbs	6 lbs

Preheat oven to 425°.

Heat the oil in a large saucepan and add the onion. Cook, stirring, over medium heat until the onion starts to brown. Add the garlic, parsley, and dill, then stir in the mustard and sugar. Do not add salt, as the feta is very salty.

If you are using fresh tomatoes, immerse them in boiling water for 30 seconds to loosen the skin and then peel. Chop the tomatoes and drain well to avoid having this dish too soupy. Add the toma-toes and tomato sauce to the saucepan and simmer for 30 minutes. If it is very watery, raise the heat a little and reduce the sauce.

Add the shrimp to the sauce and cook briefly until pink and curled. Pour the mixture into one or more large casseroles and sprinkle with the crumbled feta. Bake for 10 to 15 minutes, or until the cheese is melted. Serve with rice pilaf and green salad.

NOTE: This casserole can be refrigerated overnight and brought to room temperature before baking.

Chilaquiles

Serve this recipe as hot with peppers as you can stand it; make something else if the company won't tolerate the spice. *Chilaquiles* is a rare treat for the heat-lover.

	6	12	20	50
three-pound chickens	1	2	4	8
salt		(to taste)		
pickled hot cherry peppers	4	8	14	20
hot chilies, canned or fresh *	2	4	6	10
Italian plum tomatoes, 35-oz				
can, drained	1	2	4	8
garlic cloves	1	2	4	8
cooking oil	2 tbs	4 tbs	6 tbs	⅔ c
medium onion, chopped	1	2	4	8
chicken broth or stock	2 c	4 c	7 c	2 qts
freshly ground black pepper		(to taste)		
sharp Cheddar cheese, grated	2 c	4 c	7 c	12 c

Cook the chickens in a large preserving kettle in just enough salted water to cover for about 1 hour. (If you want a richer broth, cook chickens in canned broth instead of water.) Let the chicken cool in the broth, then remove and pull all the meat off the bones with your fingers.

If you have the time, or are doing this the day before, put the bones back in the broth and bring it to a boil, then simmer over low heat for about 2 hours. The broth will be triple-rich. You can then strain it, and use some later in the recipe. The remainder can be frozen—in ice-cube trays, then in plastic bags—for use any time.

* Note: Clean chilies and remove seeds under cold running water. Do not touch face, eyes, etc. until you have washed your hands well, and if you have any cuts on your hands bandage or cover them tightly before touching a fresh chili.

Chop the hot cherry peppers roughly and put in blender, with the chilies, tomatoes, and garlic. You will have to do this in batches, and remove the mixture to a large bowl as it is done.

In a heavy saucepan, heat the cooking oil over a medium-high flame. Add the onions and sauté, stirring, until they are golden. Turn the flame down to low and add the tomato chili-pepper mixture. Cook, stirring, for about 5 minutes, then add the chicken broth or stock and cook very slowly for about 30 minutes. The sauce should be thickish.

Toss the chicken pieces with salt and pepper. In a large casserole, make layers, beginning with the sauce, of sauce, chicken, and cheese, ending with a layer of cheese.

NOTE: The dish can be refrigerated for a day or so at this point, or kept in a cool place. It is better made a day ahead. It can be frozen, but be sure to bring it out 5 to 6 hours before heating it; if the casserole is large, the center of this dense mixture will stay frozen for a surprisingly long time.

Two hours before serving, bring to room temperature. One hour before serving, preheat the oven to 325° and bake the *chilaquiles* for 45 minutes to 1 hour [1 to 1½ hours if pans are deeper than 3 inches] until the top is bubbling and brown and the whole is heated through.

Serve with rice and red kidney beans, and *salsa fria* (a fresh pepper hot sauce) for those who demand even more "heat" to their food.

Chicken Tandoori

An Indian *tandoor* is a conical clay oven in which marinated meats are charcoal-cooked. The meat, fish, and chicken are typically bright red with spices, tangy, and dry. I have tried for ten years to reproduce the taste of the chicken *tandoori* I've had in India, and only approximate it by a combination of charcoal searing and oven baking. Some recipes call for yogurt in the marinade, but this makes it too wet, I think.

Kashmiri *mirch* is a red pepper powder; if unavailable, use Spanish paprika. *Tandoori* mixture is available at Indian spice dealers and specialty markets. Spanish paprika, used above in place of Kashmiri *mirch* is *sweet*, not hot. Hungarian paprika is obtainable sweet or hot, and if you do not use Kashmiri *mirch*, which is *hot*, here use hot Hungarian paprika or cayenne to achieve heat.

	6	12	20	50
three-pound fryer chickens	1	2	4	8
lime juice	¼ c	½ c	1 c	2 c
Kosher salt	1 tbs	2 tbs	3½ tbs	½ c

SPICES

	6	12	20	50
garlic cloves	3	6	10	20
fresh ginger, grated	2 tsp	4 tsp	7 tsp	5 tbs
freshly ground coriander seed	2 tsp	4 tsp	7 tsp	5 tbs
freshly ground cumin	1 tsp	2 tsp	4 tsp	3 tbs
cayenne	½ tsp	1 tsp	2 tsp	4 tsp
powdered aniseed or fennel seeds	¼ tsp	½ tsp	1 tsp	2 tsp
Kashmiri *mirch*	1 tbs	2 tbs	4 tbs	8 tbs
freshly ground black pepper	½ tsp	1 tsp	2 tsp	4 tsp
tandoori mixture (optional)	2 tsp	4 tsp	7 tsp	5 tbs

	6	12	20	50
peanut oil	3 tbs	6 tbs	8 tbs	1¼ c
hot Hungarian paprika	2 tbs	4 tbs	7 tbs	¾ c
or				
cayenne	1 tsp	2 tsp	1 tbs	2½ tbs

GARNISH

onion rings, thinly sliced
lime wedges

Cut the chickens into eight pieces, then wash and pat dry. Place
the pieces in a large glass, ceramic, or enameled container and toss
well with lime juice and salt. Let marinate, refrigerated, for a day
or overnight, then combine all the spices and rub into the skin of
the chicken, coating thoroughly. Marinate for another 24 hours.

Preheat the oven to 375°. If possible, sear the chicken pieces over a
very hot charcoal fire, such as a grill or hibachi. Place the chicken
pieces, preseared or not, on baking sheet[s], or in roasting pan[s]
and bake for an hour (or until done and juices run clear) basting
with the remaining marinade and the peanut oil (mixed with the
Hungarian paprika if used). Remember that this is a "dry" dish
and should not have a lot of sauce. Serve hot or cold (its good for
picnics) with lime wedges and onion rings, accompanied by *nan*
(bread baked on the inside walls of the *tandoor*) or toasted hot
Syrian bread.

Chicken Paprikash

A pungent Hungarian recipe, in which paprika, sour cream, tomatoes, and dill make a savory combination. This dish is best made with the dark meat of the chicken; the white meat tends to overcook and is also overwhelmed by the strong flavors.

Hungarian paprika is obtainable "hot" or "sweet." Use only imported.

	6	12	20	50
chicken legs and thighs	4½ lbs	9 lbs	15 lbs	30–36 lbs
small onions, minced	2	4	7	15
salt	1 tbs	2 tbs	3½ tbs	½ c
garlic cloves, finely minced	5	10	15	2 heads
fresh dill weed, finely chopped	4 tbs	8 tbs	¾ c	1½ c
or				
dried dill weed	2 tbs	4 tbs	6 tbs	¾ c
chicken stock	2 c	4 c	1½ qts	3 qts
dry, white wine	1 c	2 c	3½ c	2 bottles
sweet Hungarian paprika	4 tbs	8 tbs	¾ c	1½ c
tomato puree	¼ c	½ c	¾ c	2 c
sour cream	¾ c	1½ c	2¾ c	6 c

Place the chicken in a low, wide saucepan. Add the onion, salt, garlic, half the dill, chicken stock, and wine. Bring to a boil over high heat, then lower the heat and simmer for 20 minutes. Remove the chicken pieces from the liquid and place them in a baking pan in a 300° oven while preparing the sauce.

Skim the fat off the liquid in the pan, then reduce over very high heat by one-half. Stir in the paprika and the tomato puree and continue to cook the sauce until it thickens slightly. Remove from the heat and stir in the sour cream. Pour over the chicken, sprinkle with the remaining dill, and serve.

NOTE: If made ahead, do not put the chicken in the oven while preparing the sauce. Instead, reheat the chicken in the sauce slowly in the oven before sprinkling with the dill.

Chicken Parisienne

A "safe" casserole for crowds whose tastes are unknown. It is delicious, but no one's palate will be surprised.

If you substitute canned tomato sauce, add thyme and bay leaves.

Use Romano alone if you like, if the cost of 6 cups of Parmesan is too much. If you can buy solid Romano or Parmesan and grate it yourself, you will have a more pungent, fresher cheese.

	6	12	20	50
three-and-one-half to four-pound roasting chickens	1	2	4	8
chicken stock or water to cover	approx. 1 qt	approx. 2 qts	approx. 4 qts	approx. 6 qts
carrots, peeled and sliced	1	2	4	8
celery stalks, roughly chopped	2	4	7	8
medium onions studded with	1	2	4	8
cloves	2	4	8	16
peppercorns	12	20	35	50
salt		(to taste)		
butter	½ stick	1 stick	2 sticks	1 lb
all-purpose flour	¼ c	½ c	1 c	2 c
freshly ground black pepper		(to taste)		
heavy cream	6 fluid oz	¾ pt	1 pt, 4 liquid oz	3 pts
Tabasco		(a few drops or to taste)		
broad egg noodles	½ lb	1 lb	2 lbs	4 lbs
homemade tomato sauce	1½ c	3 c	5 c	12½ c
chives, finely chopped	3 tbs	6 tbs	10 tbs	1½ c
scallions, finely chopped	3 tbs	6 tbs	10 tbs	1½ c
egg yolks	1	2	4	8
Parmesan cheese, grated or	¾ c	1½ c	2½ c	6 c
Romano and Parmesan cheese, grated and mixed	¾ c	1½ c	2½ c	6 c

Place the chicken in a large kettle and add stock, broth, or water to cover, the carrots, celery, onion, and peppercorns. (Add salt only if water is used.) Bring to a boil and simmer for 45 minutes, or until the chicken is tender.

Remove the chicken and continue to boil the broth until it is reduced by one-half. Strain and reserve the broth. When the chicken has cooled a little, discard the skin and bones and pull the meat into strips. Set aside, moistened with a little of the broth.

Melt 2 tablespoons [4 lbs, 1 stick, ½ lb] of the butter and add the flour, stirring. When it is blended, add the reserved broth, stirring vigorously with a wire whisk. When blended and smooth, simmer over low heat, stirring occasionally, for about 30 minutes. (This is the velouté sauce.)

Preheat the oven to 350°. Melt 1 tablespoon [2 tbs, 4 tbs, 1 stick] of the butter in a skillet or large saucepan and add the chicken meat. Stir and sprinkle with salt and black pepper. Mix ½ cup [1 cup 1½ cups, 4 cups] of the cream with ½ cup [1 cup, 1½ cups, 4 cups] of the velouté. Add the Tabasco and stir this sauce into the chicken meat. Remove from the heat.

Cook the noodles in a large kettle in boiling salted water until they are tender. Do not overcook. Rinse in cold water and drain, then heat the remaining butter and toss the noodles in it.

Butter a large casserole[s], and add a layer of noodles and a layer of tomato sauce. Sprinkle with chives or scallions and spread chicken over all. Blend the remaining velouté with the remaining cream and the egg yolk[s]. Heat, until thickened, over low heat. Do not allow to boil or the eggs will scramble. Spread over the chicken and sprinkle with cheese. (At this point the dish may be set aside, cooled, and refrigerated—or kept in a very cool place overnight or for 1 or 2 days.) Bake at 350° for 45 minutes to 1 hour, or longer if the casserole is very large. The top should be golden brown and bubbly.

Chicken Bengal

A chicken curry that is simple but authentic. It should prove to you the virtue of avoiding ready-made curry powder; you can compose your own from the suggested spices. Also, you might try adding fenugreek and poppy seeds. This is a "gentle" curry, which can be made hotter by increasing the cayenne. Ready-made curry powder is often stale, as the spices were probably ground months before you buy it. The "sameness" of commercial curry powder is to me quite boring: Indian cooks make their own mixtures for each dish, of different spices and proportions. The following mixture is one I often use and can be ground in quantity in the blender and refrigerated in a screw-top jar for a week or two.

2 ounces coriander seeds
2 ounces cumin seeds
4–6 small dried red chilies
2 ounces turmeric
½ ounce cinnamon
¼ ounce cloves, whole
¼ ounce nutmeg
¼ ounce mace
2 ounces fenugreek, optional
5 pods cardamom seeds, optional

In heavy saucepan, heat all the above until they smell but are not browned. Blend together until powdered.

	6	12	20	50
frying chickens, cut into 8 serving pieces	2	4	6½	11
plain yogurt	1 c	2 c	3½ c	6½ c
garlic cloves, finely minced	2 tbs	4 tbs	7 tbs	1–2 heads
salt		(season to taste)		
cayenne, to taste, or	¼ tsp	½ tsp	1 tsp	2½ tsp
fresh ginger, finely chopped	1 tsp	2 tsp	1½ tbs	3 tbs
butter	2 tbs	4 tbs	1½ sticks	3½ sticks
cooking oil	2 tbs	4 tbs	7 tbs	1 c
onion, minced	2 c	4 c	7 c	10 c

SPICES

	6	12	20	50
cloves	3	5	8	14
ground fennel	½ tsp	1 tsp	1¾ tsp	5 tsp
ground coriander	2 tsp	4 tsp	6 tsp	10 tsp
ground turmeric	1 tsp	2 tsp	3½ tsp	7 tsp
ground cumin	½ tsp	1 tsp	1¾ tsp	5 tsp

Place the chicken in a mixing bowl [or a large preserving kettle] and add the yogurt, half the garlic, and salt and cayenne. Add the minced ginger, toss well, and let stand for at least 2 hours. (You can leave it overnight in the refrigerator.)

Melt the butter in a heavy casserole [or two large skillets]. Add the oil and onion, and cook, stirring, over medium heat until the onion is soft and golden. Add the remaining garlic and spices. Cook over low heat, stirring frequently, for about 5 minutes.

Add the chicken and marinating liquid, cover, and simmer until the chicken is tender. If the sauce is very watery, remove the chicken and keep warm while you reduce the sauce by boiling. Replace the chicken in the sauce and let cool if not serving immediately. Serve with the usual accompaniments of *raita*, pilaf, crisp pappadums, raisins, freshly grated coconut as desired (see pages 135 and 141).

NOTE: This is even better reheated and served the next day.

Couscous

Couscous, a semolina cereal, is usually steamed and has many varieties that are peculiar to different parts of North Africa and the Middle East. Couscous is traditionally made in a two-part steamer called a couscousière, which is available but not necessary, as you can improvise a steamer by lining a colander with cheesecloth, fitting it over a kettle, and covering it with a tight-fitting lid.

cheesecloth

This recipe is from Morocco (with some additions by a Tunisian friend), where the couscous is steamed and served with spicy meats and vegetables, and with a fiery-hot pepper sauce. I serve it with chicken or lamb, and often with the Sweet Meatballs that follow this recipe. This meal is very filling, so I would precede couscous only with a light soup or maybe Baba G'hanouj (page 15) with Syrian bread strips, and follow with a plain green salad and fruit. Couscous is available, in one-pound boxes, in import shops. Harissa is usually available where couscous is sold.

Harissa is a hot Moroccan pepper paste that is available in tins. It is sold in specialty shops. For a substitute, use Tabasco sauce and mashed hot chili peppers.

	6	12	20	50
couscous	1 lb	2 lbs	3 lbs	6–7 lbs
sweet butter	1 stick	2 sticks	3 sticks	6 sticks
or				
peanut oil	½ c	1 c	1½ c	3 c
boneless lamb, cut into small cubes	2 lbs	4 lbs	7 lbs	12 lbs
onions, thinly sliced	2	4	7	12
salt		(season to taste)		
freshly ground black pepper		(season to taste)		
grated fresh ginger	1 tsp	2 tsp	3½ tsp	2½ tbs
or				
ground ginger	½ tsp	1 tsp	2 tsp	1⅓ tbs
ground turmeric	1 tbs	2 tbs	3½ tsp	2½ tbs
saffron	1 tsp	2 tsp	3½ tsp	6 tsp
soaked in				
warm water	1 tbs	2 tbs	3½ tbs	6 tbs
ground cinnamon	½ tsp	1 tsp	2 tsp	4 tsp
cloves	4	6	9	18
freshly grated nutmeg	½ tsp	1 tsp	1¾ tsp	3½ tsp
potatoes	3	6	10	22
small, white turnips	2	4	7	16
carrots	3	6	10	22
20-oz cans chick-peas	1	2	3½	6
zucchini	3	6	10	22
raisins	½ c	1 c	1½ c	3½ c
almonds, blanched and slivered °	½ c	1 c	1½ c	3½ c
Harissa	2 tbs	3–4 tbs	5–7 tbs	2 cans
or				
Tabasco		(to taste)		

Place the *couscous* in a large bowl (you can use a clean plastic
dishwashing basin) and add about 2 cups [4 cups, 2 quarts, 4
quarts] cold water. Stir briefly with your fingers, then let stand 1
hour, mixing occasionally with your fingers to break up lumps.
Throughout the cooking procedure, you will have to stir the *couscous* gently to keep lumps from forming.

In the bottom of the *couscousière* kettle heat all but 2 tablespoons
butter or oil [about 4 tbs, about ¾ stick, all but ¼ pound or ½ cup]
and toss the lamb cubes into it. Add the onion and cook over low

° Eliminate if serving with Sweet Meatballs, page 66.

heat until wilted, then add the salt, pepper, and remaining spices, including the saffron and its soaking water. Then add enough water to cover all the ingredients by 2 inches. Place the top part of the pot, or the colander, over this. Line colander or top of *couscousière* with dampened doubled cheesecloth and add the *couscous*, checking once more for lumps. Cover and cook for 1 hour, checking occasionally to see that the liquid has not boiled away, and stirring occasionally.

Peel the potatoes and cut them into quarters. Also peel and quarter the white turnips. Peel the carrots and cut them into 1-inch lengths and scrub the zucchini and cut it into 1-inch lengths. Rinse and drain the canned chick-peas.

Remove the top part of the pot, stir the *couscous* again, and set the top aside. Add the potatoes, turnips, carrots, and chick-peas to the bottom and stir. Return the *couscous* and steam and cook another 20 minutes. Remove the *couscous* again, stir, and add the zucchini, raisins, and almonds, if used, to the bottom. Steam and cook for 20 minutes.

Pour the *couscous* into a large bowl and stir in the remaining butter or oil. Make a well in the center and put the stew into the hole. Serve with *harissa* in a small dish, or stir some into the stew and grain if you are sure that your guests will like a hot dish.

Sweet Meatballs for Couscous

These meatballs can also be served with pilaf and a fresh green salad for a lighter meal. They are incredibly rich and delicious; the prunes add a mysterious sweetness.

	6	12	20	50
ground lamb or beef	1½ lbs	3 lbs	5 lbs	10 lbs
onions, finely chopped	7	14	24	44
fresh parsley, finely chopped	2 tbs	4 tbs	7 tbs	1 c
eggs, lightly beaten	1	2	3	6
matzo meal	½ c	1 c	2 c	3 c
tomato paste	1 tbs	2 tbs	4 tbs	1½ 6-oz cans
salt		(season to taste)		
freshly ground black pepper		(season to taste)		
vegetable oil	4 tbs	8 tbs	12 tbs	1¼ c
water	4 c	8 c	12 c	4 qts
raisins °	½ c	1 c	1¾ c	3 c
prunes °	8	16	30	50
whole, blanched almonds	1 c	2 c	3½ c	6 c
brown sugar	½ c	1 c	1¾ c	3 c
ground cinnamon	1 tsp	2 tsp	1 tbs	2 tbs

Preheat the oven to 350°. Place the meat in a large bowl and add 1 [2, 4, 6] finely chopped onions, the parsley, egg[s], and matzo meal, then add the tomato paste, salt, and pepper. Knead well for about 5 minutes until quite smooth. Add 1 tablespoon [2 tablespoons, 4 tablespoons, 6 tablespoons] of the oil and knead again. Shape into small balls and refrigerate.

° Soak raisins in warm water for 10 minutes. Soak prunes in warm water until soft. Drain them both well before using.

In a heavy, ovenproof pan, heat the remaining oil and brown the remaining onions in it. Add the water and bring to a boil, then add salt to taste. Drop the meatballs, one at a time, into the broth and cook at a simmer until they are firm, about 8 minutes. Add the raisins, prunes, almonds, brown sugar, and cinnamon.

Bake in the oven until mahogany-colored and almost all the liquid has disappeared. Do not cover, but watch carefully at the end to make sure the meatballs do not burn.

NOTE: For large amounts, a wide, heavy pan such as a lasagne pan is best, or a wide, earthenware casserole. These reheat successfully.

Lapin Chasseur

A simple rabbit stew can be a rich and savory treat. *Fresh* thyme and parsley are especially important for this dish, as are fresh tomatoes, fresh mushrooms, and good olive oil.

	6	12	20	50
rabbits, cut into serving pieces °	1	2	4	8
olive oil	4 tbs	8 tbs	12 tbs	1½ c
onions, sliced	1	2	4	8
all-purpose flour	2 tbs	4 tbs	7 tbs	14 tbs
dry, white wine	2 c	3½ c	1½ bottles	3 bottles
bay leaves	1	2	3	6
fresh thyme, finely chopped	¼ tsp	½ tsp	1 tsp	2 tsp
parsley, finely chopped	3 sprigs	½ c	1 c	2 c
medium tomatoes, chopped	2	4	7	15
fresh mushrooms, sliced	½ lb	1 lb	1¾ lbs	4 lbs
salt		(season to taste)		
freshly ground black pepper		(season to taste)		

Preheat the oven to 325°. Brown the rabbit pieces in hot oil, in a heavy skillet. Add the onions and cook until golden, then remove the rabbit pieces and set aside. Add the flour to the oil and onions in the skillet and stir well over low heat. Add the wine, herbs, tomatoes, and mushrooms.

Place the rabbits in a large casserole and cover with the wine mixture. Cook, covered, in the oven for about 2 hours. The rabbit should not be falling off the bones.

NOTE: This casserole can be kept in a cool place, unrefrigerated, overnight. It is really excellent the next day.

° If you buy rabbit frozen, it is usually precut.

Joy Walker's Chili

This is a thick, rich chili, which should really be made ahead, at least a day and better two, before serving. It can be stretched with extra red kidney beans. Serve with fluffy rice, or just salad and crusty bread.

Coriander is available in Spanish markets, where it is called "cilantro" and in Chinese markets where it is called "Chinese parsley."

	6	12	20	50
oil	2 tbs	4 tbs	7 tbs	15 tbs
medium onions, chopped	3	6	10	24
ground beef	1 lb	2 lbs	3½ lbs	7 lbs
celery stalks, chopped	2	4	7	15
green peppers, seeded and chopped	2	4	7	15
oregano		(season to taste)		
chili powder		(season to taste)		
thyme or savory		(season to taste)		
granulated sugar	1 tsp	2 tsp	1 tbs	2½ tbs
35-oz cans Italian plum tomatoes	1	2	4	10
20-oz cans cooked red kidney beans	2	4	7	10
or				
dried red kidney beans soaked overnight and cooked until tender	¾ lb	1½ lbs	2½ lbs	4–5 lbs

GARNISH

fresh coriander bunches, chopped	1 small	2	2½	5

Heat the oil in a large kettle. Sauté the onions until golden, then add the beef, breaking up lumps as it browns. When evenly colored, add the celery, green peppers, oregano, chili powder, thyme or savory, and sugar. Add the liquid from the tomatoes and simmer, then chop the tomatoes and add them. Cook for about 30 minutes over a very low flame, stirring occasionally. Add water if the mixture is too dry.

Drain the kidney beans and rinse in a colander. Add to the kettle and cook for at least 30 minutes, again over low heat. Taste and correct the seasoning. Let cool before refrigerating and reheat slowly, adding water if needed. Serve garnished with chopped fresh coriander.

NOTE: This can be kept unrefrigerated, in a cool place, overnight.

Pork Vindaloo

A *vindaloo* is a dry and very hot Indian curry. It can be made gentler, as long as it has a "bite." The important thing is to give the pork a long marination in vinegar, to produce a "pickled" taste. Serve it with a cucumber *raita* (page 135), and a rice pilaf (page 141).

	6	12	20	50
boneless pork, cut into 1-inch cubes	2 lbs	4 lbs	7 lbs	16 lbs
salt	2 tsp	4 tsp	7 tsp	4 tbs
white wine vinegar	¼ c	½ c	¾ c	2 c
onions, finely minced	2	4	7	16
garlic cloves, finely minced	6	12	20	48
mustard seed	2 tsp	4 tsp	7 tsp	5½ tbs
ground cumin	1 tsp	2 tsp	3 tsp	7 tsp
ground turmeric	1 tsp	2 tsp	3 tsp	7 tsp
fresh ginger, finely chopped	1 tbs	2 tbs	3 tbs	7 tbs
ground cinnamon	1 tsp	2 tsp	3 tsp	7 tsp
freshly ground black pepper	¼ tsp	½ tsp	¾ tsp	2 tsp
cloves	¼ tsp	½ tsp	¾ tsp	2 tsp
cayenne (this should be HOT)		(to taste)		
butter or oil	3 tbs	6 tbs	10 tbs	1¼ c
large tomatoes, peeled and chopped	2	4	7	16
bay leaves, crumbled	2	4	7	12

Place the pork cubes in a glass or enameled bowl and mix with 2 teaspoons [4 teaspoons, 2 tablespoons, 5⅓ tablespoons] salt and the wine vinegar. Set aside.

Combine the onion and garlic with all the spices. Heat a heavy skillet (use no oil) and fry the spice mixture in it, stirring constantly, for 2 minutes. Add the spice mixture to the pork, toss well, and marinate in the refrigerator or in a cold larder for at least 24 hours. (If refrigerated, this dish improves with a 2-day marination.)

Heat the butter or oil in a heavy casserole. Add the pork and marinade, the tomatoes, and the bay leaves, and add more salt to taste if needed. Cook very slowly, covered, for about 2 hours. By the end there should not be much sauce, and the pork should be mahogany-brown but not falling apart.

Portuguese Sausage Casserole

Sausages and beans are the basis for many casseroles that can provide a hearty but inexpensive meal for a crowd. You can experiment with different kinds of sausage (*linguica,* *chorizo*—or any good garlic sausage) and beans.

	6	12	20	50
olive oil	3 tbs	6 tbs	9 tbs	1½ c
medium onions, chopped	3	6	9	24
garlic cloves, finely chopped	2	4	7	16
dried thyme	½ tsp	1 tsp	2 tsp	4 tsp
dried basil	½ tsp	1 tsp	2 tsp	4 tsp
bay leaves	2	4	7	14
35-oz cans Italian-style tomatoes	1	2	4	9
20-oz cans white kidney beans	1	2	4	9
or				
dried white kidney beans, soaked overnight and cooked until tender	½ lb	1 lb	2 lbs	5 lbs
20-oz cans chick-peas	1	2	4	9
or				
dried chick-peas, soaked overnight and cooked until tender	½ lb	1 lb	2 lbs	4 lbs
potatoes, peeled and quartered	3	6	9	24
chicken broth	1½ c	3 c	5 c	12 c
Portuguese sausages, sliced into rounds	2 lbs	4 lbs	7 lbs	16 lbs
breadcrumbs	1 c	2c	3½ c	8 c

OPTIONAL

chopped green pepper	1	2	4	10

Have all ingredients soaked, cooked, chopped, and so on, as directed above.

Heat the oil in one [or two large] casseroles. Sauté the onion over medium heat until golden and wilted. Add the garlic, thyme, basil, and bay leaves and cook another minute. Add the tomatoes and their liquid, chopping them up as you add them.

If you are using canned beans and chick-peas, drain them in a colander and run cold water through them. Add the beans and chick-peas to the casseroles along with the potatoes, then add the broth. Let cook over low heat for 20 minutes, then add the sausages and cook for another 10 minutes. Add the green pepper and cook another 15 minutes. Top the casserole with breadcrumbs and set aside (or refrigerate) until needed.

One hour before serving, place in a preheated 375° oven and heat until bubbly and brown. All the cooking, from the addition of the broth, can be done in the oven, which is especially useful if you are cooking a large amount.

NOTE: This is particularly good the next day; plan to make it ahead. It can also be kept, unrefrigerated, in a cool place.

Beef Ragoût

After watching me try several recipes for beef stew, my daughter developed this one, which is especially good because of the added orange peel. Use only the orange part: do not use white of peel as it is very bitter when cooked.

	6	12	20	50
butter	2 tbs	4 tbs	7 tbs	1 c
cooking oil	1 tbs	2 tbs	3 tbs	8 tbs
stewing beef, preferably chuck, cut into ½-inch chunks	1½ lbs	3 lbs	6 lbs	12 lbs
medium onions, sliced	2	4	7	16
all-purpose flour	2 tbs	4 tbs	7 tbs	1 c
dry, red wine	1 c	2 c	3½ c	7 c
or				
beef stock	1 c	2 c	3½ c	7 c
carrots, peeled and roughly chopped	2	4	7	16
garlic cloves, finely chopped	1	2	4	7
fresh thyme, finely chopped	1 tsp	2 tsp	1 tbs	1½ tbs
or				
dried thyme	½ tsp	1 tsp	1½ tsp	2 tsp
bay leaves	1	2	4	8
tomato paste	1 tbs	2 tbs	3½ tbs	1½ 6-oz cans
2-inch, thin strips of orange peel	2	4	7	12
peppercorns	6	12	20	40
salt	1 tsp	2 tsp	3½ tsp	2 tbs

Melt the butter and oil together in a large, heavy saucepan. Have a large casserole at hand. Over medium heat brown the meat, several pieces at a time, and as they are browned, remove them to the casserole. Add the onions to the pan and cook until soft over a medium flame.

Add the flour to the beef and toss to cover well, add the browned onions to the beef. Add the wine or stock, and bring to a simmer, stirring. Then add the carrots and the remaining ingredients. Add extra stock, wine, or water to cover all the ingredients.

Reduce the heat to very low, cover, and simmer for about 2 hours, or until the meat is soft to the touch or the fork. Do not let it cook too much or the meat will disintegrate. And watch the liquid, so that it doesn't boil away. Let the ragoût cool to room temperature, then refrigerate.

Reheat slowly and serve with whipped potatoes, boiled noodles, or rice. Or just crusty French bread and salad.

NOTE: This is 100 percent better the next day, so be sure to make it ahead.

Pollo alla Limone

A sophisticated, subtle Italian chicken dish, it should be served with Soave Bolla, a dry white wine, and accompanied by crusty bread, a simple green vegetable such as crisp green beans tossed in olive oil and garlic, and a salad. Lemon or lime is a fine adjunct to both artichokes and chicken.

	6	12	20	50
chicken, boned and cut into 2-inch pieces	3 lbs	6 lbs	10 lbs	24 lbs
all-purpose flour	2 tbs	4 tbs	7 tbs	1 c
medium onions, thinly sliced	2	4	7	16
fresh mushrooms, sliced	½ lb	1 lb	2 lbs	4½ lbs
olive oil	3 tbs	6 tbs	10 tbs	1 c plus 6 tbs
garlic cloves, mashed	2	4	7	16
dry white wine	1 c	1 bottle	2 bottles	3 bottles
chicken stock, as needed	½ c	1 c	1½ c	4 c
salt, to taste, or	½ tsp	1 tsp	2 tsp	4 tsp
freshly ground black pepper		(to taste)		
bay leaves	1	2	4	8
parsley, finely minced	2–3 tbs	4–6 tbs	¾ c	1½ c
fresh summer savory	2 sprigs	4 sprigs	⅓ c	⅔ c
or				
fresh basil	2 sprigs	4 sprigs	⅓ c	⅔ c
or				
fresh chervil	2 sprigs	4 sprigs	⅓ c	⅔ c
or				
dried basil or chervil	¼ tsp	½ tsp	1 tsp	2 tsp
lemons, thinly sliced	1–2	3–4	5–6	8–10
20-oz cans artichoke hearts, drained and rinsed	1	2	3–4	8

Dust the chicken pieces with flour and set aside. Brush mushrooms clean or rinse quickly and dry. Remove woody stems and slice the mushrooms. Sauté the onions and mushrooms in the olive oil in a large casserole. Add the garlic, then place the chicken in the casserole, mixing it with the mushrooms and onions. Add the wine and enough stock to cover the chicken. Simmer slowly, uncovered, for about 10 minutes.

Season with salt and pepper, bay leaves, parsley, and the dried herbs, if dried are used. Add the artichoke hearts and stir gently. Place the lemon slices on top, cover, and cook for another 15 minutes. Add the fresh herbs, if used, at the very end. This dish can be served on a bed of rice.

Rogan Jaush

This simple but delicious lamb curry is also called "color-passion curry." Make it hot, and add green peppers 10 minutes before the end if you like. For this it's best to grind your own spices, either in a pepper grinder, or with a mortar and pestle, or, for large amounts, in a blender.

	6	12	20	50
butter	5 tbs	10 tbs	2 sticks	5 sticks
medium onions, finely chopped	6	12	20	40
lamb (leg or shoulder) cut into 1- to 2-inch pieces	2 lbs	4 lbs	7 lbs	16 lbs
ground red chilies	½ tsp	1 tsp	1½ tsp	1 tbs
or				
cayenne	½ tsp	1 tsp	1½ tsp	1 tbs
salt		(season to taste)		
yogurt	½ c	1 c	2 c	4 c
ground coriander	1½ tbs	3 tbs	5 tbs	½ c
ground cumin	2 tsp	4 tsp	7 tsp	4⅓ tbs
fresh ginger, finely chopped	1 tbs	2 tbs	3 tbs	⅓ c
ground turmeric	1 tbs	2 tbs	3 tbs	⅓ c
ripe tomatoes, peeled, seeded, and chopped	3	6	10	22
green peppers, diced (optional)	2	4	5	12

Heat the butter in a heavy casserole. Brown the onion to an even dark brown, but do not let it burn.

Add the lamb, pushing the onion to the sides. Add the chilies (or cayenne), salt, yogurt, coriander, cumin, ginger, and turmeric. Crush the tomatoes onto the meat and cover closely. Let the meat cook at a very low simmer until the liquid is reduced. If the liquid has not reduced after 45 minutes, cook uncovered until meat is tender; the sauce should reduce to a syrupy thickness by the time the dish is done.

Serve with rice pilaf, *raita,* and chutney. Don't serve nuts and coconut with this, since the pilaf should have raisins and almonds in it.

NOTE: This is best reheated the next day.

Swedish Meatballs

The dill and wine give these meatballs extra flavor. They are excellent reheated and do well in a chafing dish for a buffet supper.

	6	12	20	50
ground chuck	1 lb	2 lbs	3½ lbs	8 lbs
ground pork and veal, mixed	1 lb	2 lbs	3½ lbs	8 lbs
white bread slices	2	4	7	15
milk	½ c	1 c	2 c	3½ c
large onions, peeled and sliced	1	2	4	9
eggs	1	2	4	9
freshly grated nutmeg	¼ tsp	½ tsp	1 tsp	2½ tsp
sweet Hungarian paprika	¼ tsp	½ tsp	1 tsp	2½ tsp
fresh dill weed, chopped	1 tbs	2 tbs	3½ tbs	½ c
salt	½ tsp	1 tsp	2 tsp	1½ tbs
freshly ground black pepper		(season to taste)		
claret or other dry red wine	¾ c	1½ c	2½ c	5½ c
butter	3 tbs	6 tbs	10 tbs	3 sticks
tomato paste	2 tbs	4 tbs	8 tbs	2 6-oz cans
all-purpose flour	3 tbs	6 tbs	10 tbs	¾ c
garlic cloves, finely minced	1	2	4	9
sour cream	1 c	1 pt	2 pts less ½ c	4½ pts
granulated sugar	1 tbs	2 tbs	4 tbs	½ c
fresh parsley, finely chopped	¼ c	½ c	¾ c	1½ c

In a large bowl [use a preserving kettle, or even a wash basin for a large recipe], combine the ground chuck, pork, and veal. In another pan, soak the bread in the milk, then squeeze dry and add to the meat. Add the onions to the meat. Beat the eggs thoroughly and add them to the meat, along with the nutmeg, paprika, salt, pepper, and ¼ cup of the wine [½ cup, ¾ cup, 1 cup]. Mix well with your hands, and shape into small balls (if for cocktails, very small). Place the meatballs on waxed paper on baking sheets and refrigerate for 1 to 2 hours. This stiffens them and makes it easier to brown them.

Heat a large, heavy skillet [two]. Add butter as needed, and when it is bubbling, add a few meatballs at a time and brown them on all sides. As they are done, remove them from the pan and place in a casserole.

After the meatballs are all browned, add the tomato paste and flour to the skillet, rubbing it in and scraping the pan as you stir. Gradually add 1½ cups water [3 cups, 5 cups, 9 cups] or more and let it bubble up. Then add the remaining wine and the garlic.

Stir and cook for 20 minutes, adding more water if too thick. (If it gets lumpy, strain through a sieve.) Remove from the heat and add the sour cream. Return the meatballs to the sauce and heat very slowly, over very low heat. Do not allow to boil. Simmer for 15 minutes, then add the sugar and parsley. Serve with boiled egg noodles and salad.

Fox Noodles

In Japan, these buckwheat *soba* noodles are often served with fried bean curd, which is said to be a favorite of the fox. With the addition of sliced Chinese sausages, they are a favorite of mine.

Soy-bean curd cakes, usually of uniform size, are available fresh or canned in Japanese markets. Japanese noodles are available in Chinese or Japanese markets or in health food stores. You may substitute no. 2 spaghetti. *Dashi* is a Japanese soup base. You can buy it at Japanese shops in the form of large "tea" bags which you infuse in boiling water. Sausages can be bought in Chinese markets. They keep, refrigerated, up to two weeks.

	6	12	20	50
tofu cakes	1	2	4	10
corn or peanut oil	½ c	1 c	1½ c	3½ c
buckwheat *soba* noodles or *udon*	1 lb	2 lbs	4 lbs	8 lbs
salt		(season to taste)		
dashi (to be authentic)	7 c	14 c	6 qts	14½ qts
or				
clear chicken broth	7 c	14 c	6 qts	14½ qts
soy sauce (use Kikkoman or imported Chinese)	3 tbs	6 tbs	10 tbs	1 c
granulated sugar	3 tbs	6 tbs	10 tbs	1 c
small Chinese pork and liver sausages	3	6	10	24
scallions, chopped with green part	2	4	8	20

Slice the *tofu* carefully into ¼-inch slices. Place on a flat board or plate and cover with waxed paper. Place a weighted plate on top to press out the liquid. (It helps to rest the plate at an angle, so that the liquid drains off.) Dry on paper towels.

Heat 1 inch of oil in a wok or heavy skillet and fry the slices, a few at a time, in very hot oil until firm and slightly browned. Remove and place on paper towels to drain.

Bring a large kettle of water to boil and add the buckwheat *soba* noodles or *udon*, stirring to separate. Boil for about 15 minutes, then drain in a colander and run cold water over them. Set them aside in the colander.

Combine 1 cup [2 cups, 1 quart, 2 quarts] of the *dashi* (or broth), the soy sauce, and sugar in a saucepan. Add salt to taste and boil until the sugar is dissolved. Add the fried *tofu* and boil for 5 minutes on high heat.

Just before serving, heat the remaining broth, add the Chinese sausages, and cook at a low simmer for 10 minutes. Put the *soba* noodles in large bowl, add the sausages and broth, then put the *tofu* and the sugar-soy mixture on top. Sprinkle the scallions over the top.

Pollo al Jerez

This is a Spanish recipe, interpreted by a Puerto Rican cook. It is important to use good sherry (not necessarily an expensive sherry) for this recipe—a medium sweet will do. It can soak into the chicken for two days, if you'd like a more pervasive sherry taste.

	6	12	20	50
three-to-four pound roasting chickens, cut into serving portions	1	2–3	4–5	8–10
sweet sherry	3 c	5 c	7 c	1½ bottles
		(more if needed)		
butter	¼ lb	½ lb	1 lb	2 lbs
tiny onions, peeled °	1 lb	2 lbs	3½ lbs	8 lbs
35-oz cans whole Italian-style plum tomatoes, drained	1	2	4	8
bay leaves	2	4	6	12
salt		(season to taste)		
freshly ground black pepper		(season to taste)		
4-oz jars pimiento-stuffed green olives, drained	½	1	2	4

Wash the chicken pieces, then pat them dry. Place the chicken in a deep glass or nonporous glazed bowl. Add the sherry, cover, and let sit overnight, or longer, in the refrigerator. When ready to cook, remove the sherried chicken from the refrigerator, and drain, reserving the sherry.

Put half the butter into a large, heavy casserole and melt it over moderate heat. Add the chicken, a few pieces at a time, and brown

---

° Drop the onions into boiling water for 10 seconds before peeling to make it easier.

on both sides. Push the browned pieces over to the sides of the casserole when you add more. When all the chicken is browned, add the remaining butter, the onions, tomatoes, bay leaves, salt, and pepper, then enough of the reserved sherry to cover the chicken and all the other ingredients. Cover and cook slowly for about 30 minutes.

Uncover, add more sherry if needed, and cook, uncovered, for another 30 minutes, or until the chicken is done. (This may also be done in a 325° oven.) Add the olives and cook to heat through.

NOTE: This can be cooled and reheated before serving.

Moussaka

Moussaka is a delicious combination of eggplant, ground meats, and tomato sauce topped with a creamy white sauce and baked until brown and bubbly. An excellent and inexpensive way to serve crowds, *moussaka* improves with a day —or even two—of waiting. You can take shortcuts with the tomato sauce by using canned tomato sauce and adding herbs such as dried basil, thyme, and oregano to taste, and simmering with salt and pepper to taste for 10 minutes or so. However, a freshly made tomato sauce makes a difference that can be noted. You may also use margarine in the béchamel and in the meat sauce, but use a good grade. The smaller amount serves 10. You will need at least three large kettles to contain sauces and mixtures for the large amount.

MOUSSAKA

	10	20	30	60
large eggplants	3	6	10	18
salt	(season to taste)			
all-purpose flour	½ c	1 c	1¾ c	2½ c
olive oil	1 c	2 c	3½ c	5 c
butter (or margarine)	6 tbs	12 tbs	3½ sticks	1½ lbs
medium onions, finely chopped	3 c	6 c	10 c	20 c
garlic cloves, minced	2	4	6	10
ground beef	1½ lbs	3 lbs	5 lbs	7 lbs
mixed with				
very lean ground lamb	1½ lbs	3 lbs	5 lbs	7 lbs
tomato sauce (page 89)	2 c	4 c	6 c	14 c
bay leaves	2	4	6	10
dried oregano	1 tbs	2 tbs	3½ tbs	8 tbs
freshly ground black pepper	(season to taste)			
red wine	2 c	4 c	6½ c	1½ bottles

	10	20	30	60
ground cinnamon	½ tsp	1 tsp	2 tsp	3½ tsp
fresh parsley, finely chopped	2 tbs	4 tbs	6 tbs	10 tbs
fresh mushrooms, sliced	10	20	¾ lb	1½ lbs
béchamel sauce (page 89)	1 qt	2 qts	3½ qts	5 qts

TOPPING

	10	20	30	60
Parmesan cheese, freshly grated	1 c	2 c	2¾ c	4 c

MOUSSAKA

Cut the eggplant into slices and sprinkle with salt. Place the slices in a large kettle and cover with water. Let stand for 30 minutes, then drain, rinse in a large colander, and dry well on paper towels. Sprinkle with flour and brown quickly, turning once, in a skillet [two or more]. Drain again on paper towels.

Heat 4 tablespoons [8 tbs, 2 sticks, 1 pound] of butter (or margarine) in a large skillet and cook the onion and garlic until golden. Add the ground meat and cook, stirring, until all the color has changed. Add the tomato sauce, bay leaves, oregano, salt and pepper to taste, wine, cinnamon, and parsley. Mix well and cook until most of the liquid has evaporated.

Sauté the mushrooms in the remaining butter (or margarine) until brown. Add to meat mixture.

Oil a roasting pan [two or more] and layer the eggplant slices with the meat mixture. Pour cooled béchamel over the top and sprinkle with the Parmesan. Bake for 1 hour [if the oven is crowded, 1½ hours], or until the top is golden brown. Let the moussaka stand about 30 minutes before serving, or cool and refrigerate until time to reheat. To reheat any such dense mixture, you should take it out of the refrigerator 2 to 4 hours before heating, to bring it to room temperature. Then heat until bubbly and heated through— 30 to 45 minutes.

TOMATO SAUCE

	10	20	30	60
medium onions, chopped	1	2	3	7
salad oil	2 tbs	4 tbs	6 tbs	⅔ c
all-purpose flour	2 tsp	4 tsp	2 tbs	4 tbs
beef or chicken stock	2 c	4 c	6 c	14 c
tomato paste	2 tbs	½ c	1½	3½
salt		(season to taste)		
freshly ground black pepper		(season to taste)		
fresh or dried thyme		(season to taste)		

Sauté the onions in the oil until golden. Add the flour, then, stirring with a whisk, add the stock and tomato paste. Simmer for 30 minutes, then add the seasonings, and simmer for 1 hour longer. Sieve or put through a food mill.

BÉCHAMEL SAUCE

	10	20	30	60
butter (or margarine)	⅓ c	½ c	1 c	2 c
all-purpose flour	⅓ c	½ c	1 c	2 c
hot milk	5 c	2½ qts	5 qts	10 qts
egg yolks	6	12	18	30
heavy cream	1 c	1 pt	1 pt and 1½ c	3 pts and 1 c
salt		(season to taste)		
freshly grated nutmeg		(season to taste)		

Melt the butter in a heavy saucepan and stir in the flour with a whisk. Add the milk and stir hard. When smooth, let simmer slowly for 20 minutes. Cool slightly.

Beat the egg yolks in a bowl, add the cream, and stir. Add a little of the hot sauce to the cream and eggs slowly, beating continuously so as not to scramble the eggs, and then add the contents of the bowl to the sauce in the pan. Stir hard and season to taste. Let cool.

Roulades Piquantes

These are beef rolls stuffed with pork and ham and braised in red wine and herbs. They are rather a job for a large crowd—not difficult, only time-consuming!—but they are delicious and make an excellent impression.

	6	12	20	50
ground pork	¾ lb	1½ lbs	2¾ lbs	6 lbs
ground ham	¼ lb	½ lb	¾ lb	2 lbs
salt	1 tsp	2 tsp	3½ tsp	5 tsp
freshly ground black pepper	1 tsp	2 tsp	3½ tsp	5 tsp
fresh parsley, finely chopped	¼ c	½ c	¾ c	1½ c
scallions, finely chopped	½ c	1 c	¾ c	3 c
brisket or chuck, sliced ¼-inch thick	2 lbs	4 lbs	7 lbs	15 lbs
olive oil	3 tbs	6 tbs	10 tbs	1¼ c
large onions, chopped	2	4	6	12
garlic cloves, minced	4	8	12	20
dry, red wine	2 c	4 c	6 c	1½ bottles
beef stock	½ c	1 c	1¾ c	4 c
tomato paste	2 tsp	4 tsp	7 tsp	1½ 6-oz cans
freshly ground black pepper	½ tsp	1 tsp	1¾ tsp	3 tsp
ground allspice	¼ tsp	½ tsp	¾ tsp	1¾ tsp

GARNISH

parsley	½ c	1 c	1¾ c	3½ c

Combine the ground meats, salt, the pepper, the parsley (except for the parsley garnish), and the scallions. Mix well with your hands, then set aside.

Place the slices of meat between two sheets of waxed paper. Pound with a mallet or an empty wine bottle so that the slices thin out and expand. Any very large slices may be halved. Spread each slice with the ground meat mixture, making a ¼-inch layer. Roll up and tie with white cotton kitchen string, or secure with a toothpick (both to be removed later). Be sure not to roll too tightly, or the filling will be squeezed out.

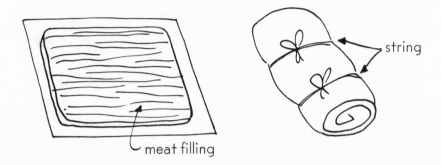

meat filling

string

Heat the olive oil in a large, heavy pot. Add the chopped onion and garlic and sauté over low heat until soft but not browned, then add the red wine. Raise the heat and boil to reduce the liquid by about one-third. Stir in the stock, tomato paste, pepper, allspice, and salt to taste. Let the sauce simmer for 30 to 45 minutes, then place the beef rolls, side by side, in it.

Simmer the beef rolls until tender (this may take 1½ hours), then remove to a platter, take out the toothpicks or strings, and return the rolls to the sauce. Reheat slowly and sprinkle with the parsley garnish before serving. The Roulades are very good served with rice and green peas.

NOTE: The beef rolls can be refrigerated after they cool. This dish is better the next day, anyway.

Stuffed Cabbage

A Middle-European staple, stuffed cabbage is memorably aromatic and delicious. It is more delicious the day after it is made.

	6	12	20	50
large white cabbages	1	2	4	8
salt pork, chopped	¼ lb	½ lb	¾ lb	2¼ lbs
medium onions, chopped	½ c	1 c	1¾ c	3¼ c
garlic cloves, chopped	1	2	4	9
dried thyme	½ tsp	1 tsp	2 tsp	4 tsp
cooked rice °	1 c	2 c	4 c	8 c
ground lean pork	1 lb	2 lbs	4 lbs	8 lbs
chicken livers	2	4	8 (about ½ lb)	16 (about 1 lb)
eggs	1	2	4	8
salt		(season to taste)		
freshly ground black pepper		(season to taste)		
fresh dill weed, chopped	1 tsp	2 tsp	4 tsp	8 tsp
fresh parsley, chopped	2 tsp	4 tsp	7 tsp	3 tbs
bacon fat or oil	2 tbs	4 tbs	7 tbs	¾ c
carrots, peeled and chopped	½ c	1 c	1¾ c	4 c
bay leaves	½	1	2	4
medium onions, finely chopped	½ c	1 c	2 c	5 c
canned Italian plum tomatoes	2 c	4 c	6 c (about 2 35-oz cans)	4 35-oz cans
sauerkraut	1 c	2 c	4 c	8 c

GARNISH

sour cream

You will need a piece of cheesecloth doubled to 12 inches by 12 inches.

° One cup of raw rice yields three cups of cooked rice.

Pull the tough outer leaves off the cabbage. Remove the tough core. Drop the cabbage into boiling water and let it cook for about 5 minutes, or until the leaves separate easily. Invert the cabbage in a colander to cool and drain.

Cook the chopped salt pork in a skillet until rendered of fat. Remove and discard the solid pieces. Add the chopped onion and garlic and cook until wilted. Add the thyme and rice and stir to blend.

Put the pork in a large bowl, add the rice mixture, and stir lightly. Finely chop the chicken livers and add them to the pork mixture. Mix in the eggs, salt, pepper, dill, and parsley.

Separate the leaves of the cabbage and pat dry, then make a V-shaped cut at the base of each leaf. Rinse out a large square of cheesecloth in cold water, then squeeze dry and place on a flat surface. Place a large leaf in the center of the cloth, curly edge up. Put a smaller leaf in the center of the first leaf and spoon 1 or 2 tablespoons of filling into its center. Bring the four corners of cheesecloth together and twist, shaping the leaves into a compact round. Remove the ball from the cloth and set aside. Repeat until the filling is used up.

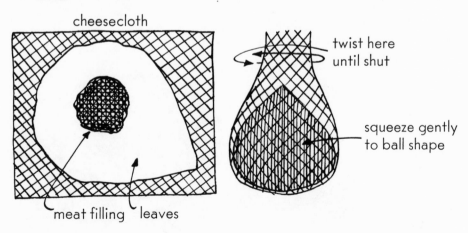

cheesecloth

twist here
until shut

squeeze gently
to ball shape

meat filling   leaves

Preheat the oven to 400°.

Heat the bacon fat in a skillet, add the chopped carrots, bay leaves, and chopped onion, and cook until the onion is wilted. Add the canned tomatoes, then sprinkle with salt and pepper and stir in the sauerkraut.

Arrange the stuffed cabbage in a neat pattern all over the sauerkraut sauce, then cover with aluminum foil. [For large amounts, use heavy-duty foil roaster pans.] Bake for 1 to 1½ hours, or refrigerate and bake before serving the next day. Serve with sour cream.

Nasi Goreng

This is a less familiar Indonesian dish than *rijstaffel*, the twenty- or thirty-dish meal served in Amsterdam and Bali. Like *rijstaffel*, *nasi goreng* is essentially rice with garnishes, but it is easier to make.

Sesame oil is available in Chinese and Japanese markets.

	6	12	20	50
chuck steak	2 lbs	4 lbs	7 lbs	12 lbs
peanut oil	¾ c	1½ c	2¾ c	5 c
garlic cloves, minced	2	4	7	12
large onions, finely chopped	2	4	7	12
ground coriander	2 tsp	4 tsp	7 tsp	4 tbs
imported curry powder	3 tbs	6 tbs	10 tbs	1 c
cayenne, to taste, or	½ tsp	1 tsp	2 tsp	4 tsp
raw shrimp, peeled and deveined	1 lb	2 lbs	3 lbs	5 lbs
scallions, chopped	½ c	1 c	2 c	4 c
chicken wings, separated into mini-drumsticks and wings	2 lbs	4 lbs	7 lbs	12 lbs
rice pilaf (page 141)				
soy sauce	¼ c	½ c	¾ c	1½ c
sesame oil	¼ tsp	1 tsp	2 tsp	4 tsp
cornstarch	¼ c	½ c	¾ c	1½ c
fresh ginger, finely minced	2 tbs	4 tbs	7 tbs	¾ c

GARNISH

egg pancakes, finely shredded				
scallions bunches, chopped	½	1	2	5
hard-boiled eggs, quartered or chopped	2	4	6	12

Cut the chuck into thin strips and place in a large mixing bowl. Combine with a little of the peanut oil, the garlic, onion, coriander, curry powder, and cayenne, and mix well. Let stand at least 1 hour.

Combine the chicken, soy sauce, sesame oil, cornstarch, and ginger and let stand 1 hour. (You can be making the egg pancakes below now.)

Put 2 tablespoons [3½ tablespoons, 5 tablespoons, 6 tablespoons] peanut oil in a wok and heat. Add the shrimp and stir-fry very quickly. After 2 minutes, add ½ cup [1 cup, 1¾ cups, 3 cups] chopped scallions. When all the shrimp are pink and curled, remove from the heat and set aside.

Wash out the wok and add 2 more tablespoons peanut oil. Heat the oil and add the beef, using more oil if needed. Cook, stirring, for 5 minutes and set aside.

Once more, clean the wok and add the remaining peanut oil. Heat and add the chicken. Cook to brown it, then lower the heat to cook through, about 15 minutes in all.

Place the rice pilaf on a large platter. Garnish decoratively with the beef, chicken, shrimp, egg pancake, and some of the following: additional chopped scallions and chopped hard-boiled eggs. Serve chutney (page 134) and *raita* (page 135) with the *nasi goreng*.

EGG PANCAKES

	6	12	20	50
eggs	5	10	16	36
all-purpose flour	2 tbs	4 tbs	7 tbs	12 tbs
granulated sugar	1 tsp	2 tsp	3½ tsp	2 tbs
soy sauce	1 tbs	2 tbs	3½ tbs	8 tbs

Combine all the ingredients and mix well. Heat a skillet and brush with oil lightly. Pour enough egg mixture to cover bottom of skillet and cook until firm over low heat. Repeat until mixture is used up. They may be stacked and then sliced into thin shreds for a garnish.

Green Enchiladas

This is a nice, easy-to-assemble casserole dish, which can be frozen or merely refrigerated for a day or two before heating. If it is cooled and stored, remember to bring it to room temperature before heating in the oven. It is good served with a green salad and fruit. The recipe came to me from Louella Williams, a great Louisiana cook whose specialties are creole.

	6	12	20	50
onions, finely chopped	2	4	7	12
butter	3 tbs	6 tbs	10 tbs	1½ c
all-purpose flour	2 tbs	4 tbs	7 tbs	1 c
milk	1 c	2 c	3 c	6 c
		(or more as needed)		
salt		(season to taste)		
freshly ground black pepper		(season to taste)		
4-oz cans green chilies, drained and finely chopped	1	2	3	6
35-oz cans tomatoes, drained and finely chopped	1	2	3	6
grated, sharp Cheddar cheese	½ lb	1 lb	2 lbs	5 lbs
fresh or frozen tortillas	30	60	100	250
vegetable oil for frying, approximately	2 c	4 c	6 c	4 qts

Sauté the onion slowly in the butter until golden and soft. Add the flour to make a paste, then let cook, stirring with a wooden spoon, for about 3 minutes. Add the milk slowly, stirring constantly until the mixture is smooth and thick. Season with salt and pepper, then add the green chilies and tomatoes. Let simmer for 5 minutes, then add the Cheddar cheese and stir well. Set aside.

Heat oil in a heavy skillet to a depth of about 1 inch. Fry the tortillas two or three at a time [use several skillets] until just heated through. Remove with tongs and dip them in the cheese mixture. Roll them up and place side by side in shallow casseroles. Pour the remaining sauce over the tortilla rolls and heat in a 325° oven for about 20 minutes, or until browned and bubbly.

Szekely Gulyas

This is an authentic Hungarian recipe that asserts the gourmet character of the best Hungarian cooking. Made from pork and sauerkraut, this goulash is delicious and can convert even the staunchest sauerkraut hater.

	6	12	20	50
boneless pork loin, cut into 1-inch cubes	1 lb	2 lbs	3¾ lbs	8 lbs
rendered pork fat or cooking oil	2 tbs	4 tbs	7 tbs	12 tbs
large onions, thinly sliced	4	8	12	24
sweet Hungarian paprika	2 tbs	4 tbs	7 tbs	¾ c
salt	1 tsp	2 tsp	4 tsp	2½ tbs
tomato puree	¼ c	½ c	¾ c	1½ c
garlic cloves, minced	2	4	7	12
caraway seeds	1½ tsp	3 tsp	5 tsp	3½ tbs
chicken stock or stock and white wine mixed	1 c	2 c	3½ c	8 c
1-lb, 13-oz cans sauerkraut, drained and rinsed with cold water	1	2	3½	4
sour cream	1 c	1 pt	2 pts less ½ c	4 pts less 1 c

In a large saucepan or skillet, brown the pork cubes in the fat or oil and set aside.

In the same skillet, brown the onions slowly until just golden. Add the pork and sprinkle with the paprika and salt, then add the tomato puree, garlic, and caraway seeds. Stir well, add the broth, and simmer, covered, for about 40 minutes. Add the sauerkraut and cook slowly until the pork is tender, about 30 minutes more.

Remove from the heat, stir in the sour cream, and reheat for 5 minutes. Do not allow the goulash to boil. Serve with small, boiled, parsleyed potatoes and a salad.

Hearty Spaghetti Sauce

This sauce is rich and thick. You can adjust the amount of tomatoes to suit your taste, but don't forget the sugar—it seems to bring out the tomato flavor. This is definitely better when made at least one day ahead.

	6	12	20	50
cooking oil	2 tbs	4 tbs	7 tbs	12 tbs
medium onions, chopped	2	4	7	16
lean, ground beef	1 lb	2 lbs	3½ lbs	8 lbs
fresh mushrooms, quartered	1 lb	2 lbs	3½ lbs	8 lbs
green peppers, seeded and chopped	2	4	7	16
35-oz cans peeled Italian tomatoes, drained and chopped	1	2	4	8
or				
28-oz cans thick tomato puree	1	2	4	8
cans of tomato paste	2	4	2	6
	6-oz	6-oz	18-oz and 1 6-oz	18-oz
garlic cloves (optional)	1	2	4	8
dried basil	1 tsp	2 tsp	4 tsp	2⅔ tbs
or				
fresh basil	½ tsp	1 tsp	2 tsp	4 tsp
dried thyme	½ tsp	1 tsp	2 tsp	4 tsp
dried oregano	½ tsp	1 tsp	2 tsp	4 tsp
granulated sugar	2 tsp	4 tsp	8 tsp	4 tbs
salt	(season to taste)			
freshly ground black pepper	(season to taste)			

Heat the oil in a heavy casserole or large skillet. Cook the onions for about 10 minutes, stirring, until they just begin to brown. Add the ground beef, stirring and breaking up lumps as it browns.

Rinse mushrooms quickly and drain. Remove tough stems of large ones. Quarter. Add the mushrooms and cook, stirring, for about 3 minutes; then add all the remaining ingredients and bring to a slow simmer. Simmer, half-covered, for about 1 hour, then taste for seasoning. If the sauce is very thin, continue to simmer, uncovered, until it thickens. Stir frequently.

Serve with plenty of linguine and grated Romano and Parmesan cheese, along with a green salad.

NOTE: This sauce can be served immediately, or it can be kept refrigerated for up to 5 days. It also freezes very well.

Pesto

Pesto is a remarkable, inimitable sauce for meats, vegetables, and, most successfully, for pasta. It is a summer mixture, because it depends on *fresh* basil—although if you are good at growing it indoors, in quantity, you can have it any time. I have never been able to grow enough indoors to have a meal of pesto without completely destroying my crop.
Serve it tossed with thin spaghetti as a main dish.

	6	12	20	50
fresh basil, packed	1 c	2 c	4 c	8 c
garlic cloves	4	8	14	30
pignolia nuts	3 ozs	6 ozs	12 ozs	24 ozs
olive oil, as needed	1 c	2 c	3¾ c	2 qts
freshly grated Parmesan cheese	½ c	1 c	2 c	4 c
salt		(season to taste)		
freshly ground black pepper		(season to taste)		

Chop the basil fine, then either pound it together with the garlic and pignolia nuts in a mortar, or place ¼ of the olive oil in the blender and then add the basil, garlic, and pignolia nuts and blend until smooth. In either case, add the Parmesan after blending or pounding and then slowly add the rest of the olive oil, as for a mayonnaise, stirring constantly, until the mixture is a thick, smooth sauce. Season with salt and freshly ground black pepper to taste. [If making pesto in a large quantity, do the blending or pounding in small batches, and mix together at the end.]

If you serve it over pasta, cook 2 pounds [4 lbs, 7 lbs, 14 lbs] of linguine to the *al dente* stage, drain it well, toss a little olive oil with the pasta to keep it from sticking, and then toss with the pesto. Serve with extra grated cheese, if desired.

Chinese Noodles with Meat Sauce

The sauce on these noodles is rich and filling. With this dish you might serve Momos (page 7) and a light pickled vegetable. It is nicest made with fresh Chinese noodles, which you can get from Chinese noodle factories or grocers, but linguine or medium spaghetti will do.

Hoisin sauce is a thick, pasty sauce made from yellow beans, and is sold here in cans in Asian groceries and specialty markets.

NOODLES AND SAUCE

	6	12	20	50
ground pork	1 c	2 c	4 c	4 lbs
dry sherry	1 tsp	2 tsp	4 tsp	2⅔ tbs
scallions, finely chopped	½ c	1 c	2 c	4 c
hoisin sauce	2 tbs	¼ c	½ c	1 c
soy sauce (Japanese Kikkoman or imported Chinese)	2 tbs	¼ c	½ c	1 c
garlic cloves, minced	3	6	10	20
Chinese noodles	1 lb	2 lbs	4 lbs	8 lbs
peanut oil	1 tbs	2 tbs	2 tbs	¼ c

GARNISHES

	6	12	20	50
medium-sized white radishes, shredded	2	4	8	16
cucumbers, shredded	½	1	2	4–6
10-oz package fresh spinach washed, picked over, parboiled in water clinging to leaves, and chopped into shreds	1	2	4	6

Combine the pork with the sherry and set aside. In a separate bowl, combine the scallions, *hoisin* sauce, soy sauce, and garlic and set aside.

Bring a large amount of water to boil in a kettle and add the noodles. If fresh, boil only 5 minutes or less (taste) and drain quickly under cold running water in a colander. If dried, cook to the *al dente* stage before draining under cold water.

Heat the cooking oil in a deep, heavy skillet or casserole. Add the pork and stir to separate; it should not be in lumps. After the pork has separated, add the scallion mixture and cook over low heat for 5 minutes, or until the sauce is thick.

Just before serving, place the garnishes in small bowls on the table. Pour boiling water over the noodles in the colander and drain well. Place the noodles in a large bowl and make a nest in the center. Pour the sauce into the nest and toss well before serving.

Beef Stifatho

There are some nice surprises in this Greek beef stew. The vinegar gives it a pleasant acid taste, the cinnamon and cumin a quite domesticated exotic savor, and the feta added just at the end so it all but melts is smooth and creamy.

	6	12	20	50
beef chuck, cut into 1-inch cubes	2 lbs	4 lbs	7 lbs	16 lbs
olive oil	2 tbs	¼ c	½ c	¾ c
large onions, chopped	1	2	5	12
bay leaves	1	2	4	6
dried oregano	pinch	½ tsp	1 tsp	1 tbs
ground cinnamon	½ tsp	1 tsp	2 tsp	2 tbs
ground cumin	½ tsp	1 tsp	2 tsp	1½ tbs
		(or to taste)		
salt		(season to taste)		
freshly ground black pepper		(season to taste)		
dry, white wine	½ c	1 c	2 c	2 qts
35-ounce cans tomato sauce	1	2	5	10
35-ounce cans Italian tomatoes	1	2	5	10
red wine vinegar	2 tbs	¼ c	½ c	1¼ c
small pearl onions, peeled	12	24	40	100
feta cheese, cubed	¼ lb	½ lb	1½ lbs	3 lbs

In a heavy skillet, brown the meat in the olive oil. Add the chopped onion and stir until it is browned, then add the herbs, spices, salt, pepper, and wine and simmer for 10 minutes. Add the tomato sauce, tomatoes, and vinegar and simmer, covered, until the meat is almost tender. If more liquid is needed, add water. If the Beef Stifatho is to be served at a later time, cool and store at this point.

When ready to serve, cook the small pearl onions in a large kettle of boiling water until almost tender. Heat the stew to bubbling, add the pearl onions, and simmer for 5 minutes, making sure the onions and the meat are tender, then add the feta cheese and simmer very slowly for 5 minutes longer, or until the cheese is hot but not really melted. Serve immediately.

Lasagne

This recipe is excellent, in that the whole recipe can be assembled as much as a day ahead and baked at the last minute. It is important, however, to bring the Lasagne to room temperature before baking to be sure it cooks through.

	6	12	20	50
35-ounce cans tomato puree	1	2	3	5
6-ounce cans tomato paste	1	2	3	4
water	1 c	2 c	3 c	5 c
dried oregano	1 tsp	2 tsp	1 tbs	3 tbs
granulated sugar	1 tsp	2 tsp	1 tbs	3 tbs
olive oil	2 tbs	¼ c	6 tbs	1 c
onions, minced	1 c	2½ c	4 c	8 c
garlic cloves, minced	1	2	4	8
ground beef	1 lb	2 lbs	3 lbs	8 lbs
salt		(to taste)		
lasagne, green is preferable	1 lb	2 lbs	3 lbs	7 lbs
mozzarella, sliced thin	1 lb	2 lbs	3 lbs	7 lbs
ricotta cheese	1 lb	2 lbs	3 lbs	7 lbs
Romano cheese, grated	¼ c	½ lb	1 lb	2 lbs

Combine the tomato puree, tomato paste, water, oregano, and sugar in a large kettle and simmer over low heat. Meanwhile, sauté the onion and garlic in a heavy skillet until golden, then add the beef and salt to taste and cook, stirring, until the beef is browned and separated. Add to the tomatoes.

Cook the lasagne in a large kettle of boiling water, stirring to see that it does not stick. [In large amounts, best to do it in batches.] As it comes to the *al dente* stage, drain in a colander, run cold water over it, and toss in a large pot with oil, to keep it from sticking.

Grease a large casserole or large baking pans and layer the lasagne, tomato sauce, ricotta, and mozzarella, with Romano sprinkled on every other layer, and finishing with ricotta and Romano. Bake at 375° for 30 minutes.

NOTE: This can be covered with foil and stored in the refrigerator before baking. Also, larger pans may take more cooking time, depending on the depth of the layers.

Carbonnades Flamandes

The distinctive taste of this Belgian beef stew comes from the addition of beer or ale. You should also try the Irish version of it, made with Guinness stout.

	6	12	20	50
lean chuck or rump	3 lbs	6 lbs	10 lbs	24 lbs
cooking oil	2 tbs	4 tbs	7 tbs	1 c
medium onions, sliced	1½ lbs	3 lbs	6 lbs	12 lbs
salt	(season to taste)			
freshly ground black pepper	(season to taste)			
garlic cloves, mashed	4	8	12	24
beef stock or bouillon	1 c	2 c	4 c	8 c
ale or beer	2–3 c	4 c	6 c	4–6 12-oz cans
brown sugar	2 tbs	¼ c	½ c	1 c
bouquet garni * composed of				
parsley	2 sprigs	4 sprigs	7 sprigs	½ bunch
bay leaves	1	2	3	6
dried thyme or	1 tsp	2 tsp	3 tsp	2 tbs
fresh thyme	2 sprigs	4 sprigs	7 sprigs	15 sprigs
cornstarch mixed with	2 tbs	4 tbs	8 tbs	1 c
wine vinegar	2 tbs	4 tbs	8 tbs	1 c

GARNISH

parsley	6 sprigs	12 sprigs	1 bunch	2 bunches

Preheat the oven to 325°.

* Tie the three herbs in a small square of cheesecloth.

Cut the beef into 4 × ½ × 2-inch strips. Pat the strips dry, then heat the oil in a skillet and brown the beef quickly, a few strips at a time. Place the strips in a bowl as they are done.

When all the beef is browned, reduce the heat under the skillet, add the onions, and cook for 10 minutes, stirring. Season with salt and pepper, then stir in the garlic.

Sprinkle the beef with salt and pepper, then layer it in the casserole with the onions.

Heat the stock in the skillet, scraping up the pan juices and add to the meat. Add just enough beer or ale to cover, then stir in the brown sugar and bouquet garni. Bring the casserole to a simmer on top of the stove, then cover and place in the oven. Keep the casserole simmering for 1½ to 3 hours [large casseroles may take longer] or until the meat is tender.

Remove the bouquet garni and discard. Drain the liquid out of the casserole and skim the fat off it. Beat the cornstarch and vinegar mixture into the liquid, and simmer for 4 minutes or so in a saucepan. Taste, correct the seasonings, then pour the sauce back over the meat. (If it doesn't seem thick enough, add more cornstarch mixed with water and simmer again). Set aside until ready to serve, then heat through for 5 minutes or so.

Serve with noodles or boiled potatoes, and garnish with parsley.

Dirty Rice

This is a fine, inexpensive way to serve a lot of people. I received this recipe from Gladys Glaude of Carencro, Louisiana, who patiently explained her ways with spices and gumbos, crayfish and dumplings. Mrs. Glaude and her sister Louella Williams are well-known Louisiana cooks. Louella Williams shared many recipes with me, including Green Enchiladas, page 98.

I don't know why this rice is "dirty": it seems that it has always had that name, over a wide area of the South. It does have a motley appearance.

	6	12	20	50
olive oil	5 tbs	½ c	1 c	2½ c
all-purpose flour	2 tbs	4 tbs	½ c	1 c
beef stock or bouillon	3 c	6 c	2¼ qts	4 qts less 1 cup
large onions, finely chopped	1	2	4	10
celery stalks, diced small	1	2	4	10
large green peppers, diced	1	2	4	10
garlic cloves, minced	4	8	12	24
Tabasco	(season to taste)			
lean beef ground with	1 lb	2 lbs	3½ lbs	5½ lbs
beef liver	1 lb	2 lbs	3½ lbs	5½ lbs
raw, long-grain converted rice	2–3 c	4–5 c (or 2– 2½ lbs)	8–9 c (or 4– 4½ lbs)	10–12 c (or 5– 6 lbs)
4-oz jars pimientos, drained and diced	½	1	2	4
salt	(season to taste)			
freshly ground black pepper	(season to taste)			

In a heavy skillet, heat 3 tablespoons [6 tablespoons, ½ cup, ¾ cup] of the olive oil and add the flour, stirring well. Let cook, stirring, until well browned. Add the beef stock or bouillon and stir well while you bring the mixture to a boil. Let the *roux* simmer over a low flame for 20 minutes or so.

Meanwhile, heat the remaining oil in a large kettle. Add the onion, celery, and green pepper and sauté over medium heat, stirring, until tender and the onion is golden. Add the minced garlic, Tabasco, and beef and liver.

Stirring well to separate the meat, sauté until the meat turns color. Add the *roux* mixture from the skillet and cook for 15 minutes over low heat, then add the rice and cover. Cook over low heat for 15 minutes, then uncover and add water if the liquid has been absorbed. Cook another 10 minutes, then toss the mixture lightly with the diced pimiento and season with salt and pepper to taste.

Dirty Rice is good with corn on the cob and a green salad.

Cocido Valenciana

This is a Spanish version of a boiled dinner, superior, in my view, to the New England variety. It is the recipe of Vicente de Crespo of Denia, Spain, and was given to me by Trin Yarborough. The bright yellow coloring and rough chunks of vegetables and meats inspire a hearty appetite. Serve it with rice and a big, garlicky salad.

	6	12	20	50
stewing beef, such as chuck	2 lbs	4 lbs	7 lbs	12 lbs
olive oil	3 tbs	6 tbs	10 tbs	1¼ c
cow knee bone, or other marrow bones	1–2 lbs	2–4 lbs	3–5 lbs	6–10 lbs
small turnips, peeled and halved	6	12	20	45
carrots, scraped and quartered	4	8	12	30
parsnips, peeled and chunked	3	6	10	24
saffron	¼ tsp	½ tsp	1 tsp	2¼ tsp
or				
turmeric	2 tsp	4 tsp	1½ tbs	5 tbs
or				
achiote seeds	1 tbs	2 tbs	1¾ tbs	4½ tbs
medium potatoes, peeled and chunked	4	8	12	30
20-oz cans cooked chick-peas	1	2	3	6
heads of white cabbage, chunked	½	1	2½	5
salt	(season to taste)			
freshly ground pepper	(season to taste)			

If you use the achiote (available in Spanish markets), heat the seeds in the olive oil until it is a bright yellow and then discard the seeds.

Cut the stew meat into rough chunks and brown it in the olive oil in a heavy skillet. Add water just to cover. [If making a large amount, place the meat in a large casserole before adding the water.] Add the turnips, carrots, and saffron or turmeric (if you have not used the achiote method for coloring). Add salt to taste, then bring the stew to a boil. Lower heat and simmer, covered, for 1 hour.

Then add the rest of the vegetables, cut in large chunks, and cook for about 20 more minutes, until all are tender. Season to taste.

NOTE: The broth may be served separately as a soup, with garlic croutons in it.

Pavo Estofado

A "smothered turkey" can be a fine, exotic change from the usual stuffed and roasted bird. You can make all kinds of substitutions for the ingredients—raisins for the prunes, small, pickled green peppers for the olives, and so on—or you can leave out any of the above. This Caribbean dish is quite a hearty one.

To facilitate peeling the onions and the garlic, drop them in boiling water for 10 seconds and drain them in a colander.

	6	12	20	50
garlic	6 cloves plus 1 head	12 cloves plus 2 heads	4 heads	7 heads
peppercorns	12	24	32	45
oregano	5 tsp	3 tbs	5 tbs	8 tbs
salt	3 tbs	6 tbs	9 tbs	1 c
vinegar	2 tbs	4 tbs	7 tbs	¾ c
8-to-10-pound turkeys, cut into pieces	1	2	4	6–7
dry prunes, pitted	12	24	40	2–3 12-oz boxes
small onions, peeled	1 lb	2 lbs	3½ lbs	7 lbs
bay leaves	4	8	12	24
green olives	12	24	40	50
capers	2 tbs	4 tbs	7 tbs	2 medium bottles
liquid from capers	1 tbs	2 tbs	4 tbs	9 tbs
dry, red wine	½ c	1 c	2 c	4 c
granulated sugar	¾ c	1½ c	2½ c	4 c

Combine the 6 cloves [12 cloves, 1 head, 2 heads] garlic, peppercorns, oregano, salt, and vinegar in the blender, or grind in a mortar and pestle. Put the turkey pieces in a large kettle and rub well with the blended ingredients. Refrigerate overnight.

The next day add all the other ingredients, including the rest of the garlic, except for the wine and sugar and cook over high heat for 10 minutes, to bring to a boil. Then reduce the heat to moderate and cook for 2 hours.

Add the wine and sugar and reduce the heat to very low. Simmer, covered, for 30 minutes to 1 hour more, or until the turkey is tender.

VEGETABLES
AND
SIDE DISHES

Chinese Spiced Eggplant

This has been called a Chinese *ratatouille*, and it bears some resemblance to the French dish, in that it is excellent cold or hot (best, I think, at room temperature). The oily and succulent eggplant, the crunch of sesame seeds, and the savor of garlic provide a wonderful combination. The recipe is included through the kindness of Phebe Chao.

Sesame oil and chili paste are available in Chinese and Japanese markets.

	6	12	20	50
medium eggplants	2	4	7	16
soy sauce (imported Japanese or Chinese)	3 tbs	6 tbs	½ c plus 3 tbs	1 c plus 9 tbs
red wine vinegar	2 tbs	4 tbs	7 tbs	1 c
granulated sugar	2 tbs	4 tbs	7 tbs	1 c
salt	¼ tsp	½ tsp	1 tsp	2½ tsp
sesame oil	2 tsp	4 tsp	7 tsp	5 tbs
peanut oil (really the best for Chinese cooking)	1 tbs	2 tbs	3½ tbs	7 tbs
garlic, finely chopped	1 tbs	2 tbs	3½ tbs	7 tbs
ginger, peeled and finely chopped	2 tbs	4 tbs	7 tbs	½ c
fresh green chilies, finely chopped and seeds removed	1	2	4	8
green sweet peppers, finely chopped and seeds removed	1	2	4	8
chili paste with garlic (optional)	1 tsp	2 tsp	3½ tsp	6 tsp
white sesame seeds	1 tbs	2 tbs	3½ tbs	8 tbs

Wash the eggplant and trim off stems. Steam for at least 30 minutes in a colander over simmering water, covered, or in a large vegetable steamer or Chinese bamboo steamer. When the eggplants are soft through and collapsed, they are finished. Let them cool on a platter.

Combine the soy sauce, vinegar, sugar, salt, and sesame oil and set aside. Heat the peanut oil in a wok or heavy skillet and sauté the garlic, ginger, chili pepper, and green pepper in it, very quickly, stirring constantly. Add the chili paste, if used, then add this mixture to the soy mixture. Bring to the boil, then remove from the heat and cool.

Toast the sesame seeds in a dry heavy skillet just until they pop. Do not let them get brown. Cool and set aside. Peel the eggplant and chop roughly. Place in a serving bowl and pour the sauce over, tossing well. Sprinkle with sesame seeds before serving.

NOTE: You can make this ahead by a day or two, and bring it to room temperature before serving. It can also be kept, unrefrigerated, in a cool place.

Sicilian Broccoli

Broccoli is fast becoming one of my favorite vegetables. It must be slightly undercooked, however, to be good at all. I think most vegetables should be undercooked. Parboil this ahead of time, and reheat briefly with oil, wine, and garlic. This is good as a first course, or a separate vegetable course.

	6	12	20	50
broccoli, separated into florets and ends peeled	2 lbs	4 lbs	7 lbs	16 lbs
olive oil	5 tbs	½ c plus 2 tbs	1¼ c	2½ c
garlic cloves, finely chopped	2	4	8	15
salt		(season to taste)		
freshly ground black pepper		(season to taste)		
dry, white wine	2 c	1 qt	1¾ qts	2½ qts

Wash and drain the broccoli. In a very large pot, parboil it in a large amount of water for 4 to 5 minutes. Immediately drain the broccoli, run cold water over it, and set aside until serving time.

Heat the olive oil in a large skillet or wok [or two] and sauté the garlic, being careful not to burn it. Add the wine, salt, and pepper and boil until the wine reduces by about one-half. Just before serving, heat the wine to bubbling and toss the broccoli in it until heated through.

Bean Sprout Salad

This is an excellent picnic food. It can be eaten in halves of Syrian bread, or as an accompaniment to grilled foods. Good, too, with a Chinese meal, though scarcely authentic. It is an adaptation of a Southeast Asian (Thai) dish.

	6	12	20	50
fresh bean sprouts	1 lb	2 lbs	3 lbs	8 lbs
soy sauce (Japanese Kikkoman or imported Chinese)	2 tbs	¼ c	6 tbs	¾ c
rice wine vinegar	2 tbs	¼ c	6 tbs	½ c
sesame oil	2 tbs	¼ c	6 tbs	½ c
cucumbers, peeled, seeded, and chopped	1	2	3	8
scallion bunches, chopped	1	2	3½	8
small white radishes, cleaned and chopped	2	4	8	16
freshly ground black pepper	2 tsp	4 tsp	8 tsp	5⅓ tbs

GARNISH

	6	12	20	50
fresh parsley	1 tbs	2 tbs	3 tbs	7 tbs
cooked and peeled shrimp (optional)	½ lb	1 lb	1½ lbs	4 lbs

Pick over the bean sprouts, wash quickly, and drain in a colander. Pour boiling water over them in the colander, then run cold water over to cool them.

Combine the bean sprouts, cucumber, scallions, and radishes in a large bowl, then chill. Before serving, toss with the soy sauce, vinegar, and sesame oil, and season with black pepper. If desired, garnish with parsley and cooked shrimp.

Tomatoes Provençale

A splendid way to improve tasteless supermarket tomatoes. This fresh and garlicky dish complements grilled or roasted meats.

	6	12	20	50
tomatoes	6	12	20	50
salt		(season to taste)		
freshly ground black pepper		(season to taste)		
fresh breadcrumbs *	⅓ c	⅔ c	1⅓ c	3 c
garlic cloves, finely minced	1	2	4	8
scallions, green part and all, finely chopped	2 tbs	4 tbs	7 tbs	1 c
fresh parsley, finely minced	3 tbs	6 tbs	10 tbs	2½ c
dried thyme	pinch	1 tsp	1¾ tsp	1 tbs
olive oil	3 tbs	9 tbs	1 c	2½ c

Remove stem and cut each tomato in half, horizontally, and gently squeeze, cut side down, to remove excess juice and seeds. Sprinkle each tomato half with salt and pepper.

Preheat the oven to 400°.

Combine all the remaining ingredients except 1 tablespoon [2 table-spoons, 3½ tablespoons, ⅔ cup] of the olive oil. Place the tomatoes in a greased baking dish [or greased roaster pans] and stuff each with the herb-breadcrumb mixture. Sprinkle with the remaining olive oil and bake for about 15 minutes.

NOTE: The tomatoes may be prepared for baking and stored over-night. Bake just before serving.

* Fresh breadcrumbs can easily be made in a blender. The crust may be included.

Ratatouille

Ratatouille is the classic French vegetable stew. Like other stews, it is especially good made the day before, and it can be served hot or cold. Serve cold with lemon wedges. Also, if you serve it cold, it may need more salt than if you serve it hot.

	6	12	20	50
medium eggplants, cut into 1½-inch cubes	1	2	4	8
medium zucchini, quartered and cut into 1-inch lengths	3	6	10	18
salt		(season to taste)		
olive oil	6 tbs	12 tbs	1¼ c	2 c
freshly ground black pepper		(season to taste)		
onions, coarsely chopped	3	6	10	18–20
green peppers, seeded, cored and coarsely chopped	2	4	7	12
garlic cloves, finely minced	4	8	16	24
bay leaves	1	2	4	8
fresh tomatoes, peeled and cut into eighths	2 lbs	4 lbs	7 lbs	12 lbs
or				
35-oz cans Italian plum tomatoes, drained	1	2	3	6
fresh parsley, finely chopped	½ c	1 c	1¾ c	3½ c
fresh thyme, finely chopped	2 tsp	4 tsp	7 tsp	4 tbs
or				
dried thyme	½ tsp	1 tsp	1 tbs	2 tbs
fresh basil, finely chopped	1 tbs	2 tbs	3½ tbs	7 tbs
or				
dried basil	1 tsp	2 tsp	3½ tsp	7 tsp

Place the eggplant and zucchini in a colander, then set in a large bowl or kettle and salt lightly. Toss well and set aside for 1 hour, then rinse and pat dry with towels.

Heat half the oil in a large skillet and add the eggplant, zucchini, and freshly ground pepper. Sauté for about 5 minutes, stirring.

In a large skillet or casserole, heat the remaining oil and add the onion and green peppers. Add the garlic and bay leaves, then add the tomatoes and simmer for 10 minutes. Add the eggplant-zucchini mixture, parsley, thyme, and basil, and stir well. Simmer, covered, on top of the stove for 20 minutes, or until the vegetables are tender.

NOTE: This dish can also be baked in a 325° oven until tender. It can be kept, unrefrigerated, in a cool place.

Artichokes and Chick-peas Vinaigrette

This is an elegant, yet hearty, cold salad, which would go well with broiled foods or a roast. It was last served at a mock Roman orgy, beside an entree of squab with truffled paté stuffing—but it would be excellent with charcoal-broiled hamburger!

	6	12	20	50
10-oz packages frozen artichoke hearts	2	3	4	6
or				
20-oz cans, drained and rinsed	2	3	4	6
20-oz cans cooked chick-peas, drained and rinsed	2	3	5	10
medium red onions, finely chopped	1	2	4	8
chopped fresh herbs, as available, such as				
fresh basil	1 tbs	2 tbs	3½ tbs	7½ tbs
fresh thyme	½ tbs	1 tbs	1½ tbs	3½ tbs
fresh parsley	1 tbs	2 tbs	3½ tbs	7½ tbs
fresh chives	½ tbs	1 tbs	1½ tbs	3½ tbs
salt	(season to taste)			
freshly ground black pepper	(season to taste)			

DRESSING

Garlic French Dressing on page 130.

If you are using frozen artichoke hearts, partially thaw them, to separate them, and then put them into a saucepan full of boiling water for 3 minutes. Drain and run cold water over them. If you are using canned artichokes, put them in a colander and rinse them well with cold water, to remove any briny taste. (If they were packed in oil, drain only). Toss all the ingredients together in a serving bowl and refrigerate for 2 or 3 hours before serving.

Orange-Red Onion-Cress Salad

For the times when green salad, unadorned, begins to pall, this refreshing and colorful combination will encourage appetites.

	6	12	20	50
large heads romaine lettuce	2	4	6	8
watercress bunches	2	4	6	8
large navel oranges, peeled and thinly sliced	1	2	3	7
onion rings, thinly sliced	1 c	2 c	3 c	5 c

DRESSING

Garlic French Dressing on page 130.

Wash the lettuce and watercress. Drain very well and pat dry between towels. [For large amounts, I use a double thickness of bedsheet over a large table, or even a clean floor.] Be sure the lettuce and cress are clean and dry, then pick over and tear into bite-sized pieces. Place in a salad bowl. [For large amounts, keep the greens in plastic garbage bags until needed.] Just before serving, add the oranges and onion rings and toss well with the dressing.

Garlic French Dressing

The amount for six is perhaps more than you might need for one service, but it keeps, covered, in the refrigerator for about ten days. Let it come to room temperature before dressing a salad.

You may add lemon juice to your taste. I like it quite lemony.

	6	12	20	50
dry mustard	1 tsp	2 tsp	3¾ tsp	8 tsp
water	1 tbs	2 tbs	3¾ tbs	8 tbs
garlic cloves, finely minced	1	2	3	5
granulated sugar	1 tsp	2 tsp	3½ tsp	5 tsp
salt	1 tsp	2 tsp	3½ tsp	5 tsp
olive oil °	1 c	2 c	3½ c	5 c
lemon juice	3 tbs	6 tbs	10 tbs	1½ c
grated onion (optional)	1 tsp	2 tsp	3½ tsp	5 tsp

Combine the mustard with the water and let stand 10 minutes. Mix in the garlic, sugar, salt, and oil and let stand for 1 hour. Add the lemon juice and grated onion, if desired, pour into a large jar, and beat or shake very well. Dress the salad just before serving.

° Use inexpensive pure olive oil—such as A&P brand—as it often has more olive taste than the more refined and expensive.

Tabbouleh

This is an unusual, lemony cracked wheat salad, excellent for
crowds and easy to prepare. The cracked wheat is soaked
until tender and mixed with herbs and vegetables.

	6	12	20	50
bulghar wheat (or cracked wheat)	1 c	2 c	3½ c	8 c
onions, finely chopped	¾ c	1½ c	2¾ c	6 c
scallions, finely chopped	½ c	1 c	1¾ c	4¼ c
salt	1 tsp	2 tsp	3¾ tsp	6 tsp
freshly ground black pepper	¼ tsp	½ tsp	¾ tsp	1¾ tsp
Italian parsley, finely chopped	1½ c	3 c	5 c	10 c
fresh mint leaves, finely chopped	½ c	1 c	1¾ c	4 c
or				
dried mint	3 tbs	6 tbs	10 tbs	1 c
lemon juice	½ c	1 c	1¾ c	4 c
olive oil	¾ c	1½ c	2¾ c	6 c

GARNISH

tomatoes, peeled and chopped	2	4	6	12

Cover the wheat with cold water and let stand for 1 hour. Make
sure you have put it in a very large pot, as it expands enormously.
Drain, then squeeze out the extra water with your hands. Add all
the remaining ingredients except the tomatoes and mix with your
hands. Place in a large bowl and garnish with the tomatoes.

NOTE: This can be made the day before and refrigerated.

Rice Salad

Rice salad is unusual and refreshing, and a good picnic accompaniment to grilled foods.

	6	12	20	50
raw, converted rice	2 c	4 c	6 c	12 c
salt		(season to taste)		
fresh ginger slices	2	4	6	12
raisins	½ c	1 c	1¾ c	4 c
freshly ground black pepper		(season to taste)		
ground cumin	½ tsp	1 tsp	2 tsp	4 tsp
olive oil, as needed	¼ c	½ c	1 c	2¼ c
lemon juice		(season to taste)		
blanched, slivered almonds		(to taste)		
dried apricots and prunes *	½ c	1 c	1¾ c	4 c
scallions, chopped	½ c	1 c	1¾ c	4 c

Boil the rice in salted water, with the ginger slices, for about 15 minutes: the rice should not be soft, but just firm, *al dente*. Drain carefully, then remove the ginger slices. You can chop them fine, if you like ginger, and add to the rice later.

While the rice is still warm, season it with freshly ground black pepper, a little salt, the cumin, and raisins. Add just enough olive oil to make it shiny; it should not be heavily "dressed." Add lemon juice to taste.

When the salad is cool, add the almonds and apricots and prunes, and stir in scallions. Serve at room temperature—not ice-cold.

NOTE: This can be kept, unrefrigerated, in a cool place.

* Soak in boiling water for 10 minutes, then drain and chop.

Kishmish Chutney

This is a very sweet tomato and raisin chutney, of a pleasing reddish mahogany color. It is unusual in that you can either serve it the same day it is made or store it in the refrigerator for a month or two.

	6	12	20	50
butter	2 tbs	4 tbs	1 stick	2 sticks
seedless raisins	½ lb	1 lb	1¾ lbs	3½ lbs
medium tomatoes, peeled and chopped	3	6	10	25
water	½ c	1 c	1¾ c	3½ c
		(or as needed)		
whole cloves	2	4	7	10
cinnamon sticks	1	2	4	8
salt	1 tsp	2 tsp	3½ tsp	3 tbs
freshly ground black pepper		(season	to taste)	
granulated sugar	½ c	1 c	1¾ c	3¼ c
wine vinegar	1½ tbs	3 tbs	5 tbs	12 tbs

Melt the butter in a saucepan and toss in the raisins. Cook for 2 minutes, then add the tomatoes and cook over medium heat, uncovered, for 7 minutes. Stir constantly.

Transfer either to a double boiler or to a very heavy casserole and add the water, cloves, cinnamon, salt, and pepper. Mix well and cook very slowly, uncovered, for 1 hour, stirring occasionally. Add the sugar and vinegar and cook for 30 minutes more. If needed, add more water while cooking. Let cool, and, if not to be used the same day, put in canning jars.

Banana and Cucumber Raitas

Raitas are served with curries to cool the palate. You can make raita with other vegetables as well.
See also the recipe for Tomato Pachadi, page 137.
The yogurt amounts for the banana raita are approximate, the banana taste goes very far.

BANANA RAITA

	6	12	20	50
plain yogurt	1 pt	4 c	7 c	12 c
ripe bananas	2	4	7	12
cardamom pods	2	4	7	12

Place the yogurt in a large bowl. Peel the bananas and squeeze them through your hands to make a rough puree. Add to the yogurt and mix. Crush the cardamom and extract the black seeds. Pound them a little in a mortar and add to the yogurt. Let stand for a few hours or overnight, to develop the flavor. This will keep for a day or so.

CUCUMBER RAITA

	6	12	20	50
large cucumbers	1	2	4	8
salt	½ tsp	1 tsp	2 tsp	4 tsp
scallions, finely chopped	2	4	8	16
caraway seeds	(season to taste)			
plain yogurt	2 c	4 c	8 c	12 c

Peel the cucumbers, slice in half lengthwise, and scoop out the pulpy seeds with a spoon, leaving you with boat-shaped halves.

Using the largest holes of the grater, grate the cucumber into a bowl. Add the salt, stir, and let sit for 2 hours.

Drain the cucumbers in a colander, then press out as much water as possible. Add the chopped scallions and caraway seeds. Just before serving, add the cucumber to the yogurt in a large bowl. This will keep only a day or two, and might get watery from the juices the cucumber exudes.

Tomato Pachadi

This is a condiment, to be served with Indian and Nepali meals. It is cool and refreshing, like the *raitas*.

	6	12	20	50
ripe tomatoes, peeled, seeded, and chopped	2 c	4 c	7 c	12 c
medium onions, finely chopped	1	2	4	8
4-oz cans pickled green chilies	½	1	1½	2½
or				
fresh green chilies, finely chopped	1	2	3	4
fresh coriander, finely chopped	2 tbs	4 tbs	7 tbs	15 tbs
salt	½ tsp	1 tsp	2 tsp	4 tsp
plain yogurt	1 c	2 c	4 c	2 qts

GARNISH

green peppers, finely chopped	1	2	3	4

Combine all the ingredients except the yogurt and the green pepper and mix well. Refrigerate. Just before serving, drain the tomato mixture, which will have accumulated water, and add the yogurt. Taste for seasoning, garnish with the green pepper, and serve.

NOTE: This will keep refrigerated for two or three days.

Potato Achar

This is a traditional Nepali side dish, a sort of fresh "pickle" that is served at room temperature. It is excellent on the second or third day.

Mustard oil is available in specialty markets.

	6	12	20	50
medium potatoes, peeled and quartered	6	12	20	48
mustard or peanut oil	½ c	1 c	1¾ c	3½ c
mustard seeds	2 tbs	¼ c	½ c	1 c
white sesame seeds	½ c	1 c	1¾ c	3½ c
chili powder	2 tbs	¼ c	½ c	1 c
fresh ginger, finely chopped	1 tsp	2 tsp	3¾ tsp	8 tsp
coarse salt		(season to taste)		
lime or lemon juice, to taste	1 tbs	2 tbs	3½ tbs	⅓ c

GARNISH

	6	12	20	50
fresh coriander, finely chopped or	½ c	1 c	2¾ c	4 c
ground coriander	2 tsp	4 tsp	7 tsp	5 tbs

Boil the potatoes for 10 to 15 minutes, until cooked through but not mushy. Drain and set aside.

Heat the oil in a heavy skillet and add the mustard seeds, sesame seeds, chili powder, and chopped ginger. Cook, stirring, for 4 minutes.

Put the potatoes in a large bowl and toss with the cooked spice mixture. Salt to taste, and add the lime or lemon juice. Garnish, when cool, with fresh coriander, or toss with ground coriander.

NOTE: This can be kept, unrefrigerated, in a cool place.

Dhal

This is a lentil curry that, with rice, forms the staple of the Nepalese diet. It is high in protein and smooth and rich in taste. Best made ahead, it thickens with standing and must be thinned with more stock or water. Reheat slowly, as it can stick and burn.

Clarified butter is made by heating butter and letting the milky solids separate from the clear yellow liquid, and then by skimming or straining through cheesecloth to remove the milky solids. Indian *ghee* can be bought tinned in Indian groceries.

	6	12	20	50
dried red lentils	2 c	1 lb, 4 ozs	3 lbs	6 lbs, 2 ozs
chicken broth, canned or home-made, to cover lentils	2½ c	1¼ qts	2½ qts	4 qts
garlic cloves, chopped	1	2	3	5
medium onions, chopped	2	4	7	12
vegetable oil or clarified butter (*ghee*)	2 tbs	4 tbs	7 tbs	1 c
bay leaves	1	2	4	8
ground cumin	1 tsp	2 tsp	4 tsp	8 tsp
ground coriander	1 tsp	2 tsp	4 tsp	8 tsp
ground fennel	1 tsp	2 tsp	4 tsp	8 tsp
hot paprika	1 tbs	2 tbs	4 tbs	½ c
ground turmeric	1 tsp	2 tsp	4 tsp	8 tsp
crushed red pepper	½ tsp	1 tsp	2 tsp	4 tsp
salt		(season to taste)		

GARNISH

fried onions
toasted almonds
raisins

Soak the lentils in cold water for about 1 hour. Drain and place in heavy saucepan with enough chicken broth to cover. Simmer slowly, stirring occasionally.

Meanwhile, heat the oil or butter in a heavy skillet and gently sauté the onion and garlic until golden. Add the bay leaves and all the spices and stir over medium heat for 3 to 4 minutes. Add the mixture to the lentils and stir. Add water or more broth if the liquid has been absorbed. Cook over low heat, for 45 minutes to one hour, stirring occasionally, and adding liquid whenever needed. When the lentils are mushy and cooked through, the *dhal* is done. Add salt to taste.

NOTE: You can garnish *dhal* with fried onions, toasted almonds, and raisins plumped in butter, or chopped fresh coriander, for an authentic touch. The dish can also be kept, unrefrigerated, in a cool place.

Orange Rice Pilaf

The addition of orange juice makes this recipe for pilaf something special.

	6	12	20	50
raw, long-grain rice	2 c	4 c	2 lbs, 6 ozs	5 lbs, 5 ozs
butter	3 tbs	6 tbs	10 tbs	3 sticks
6-oz cans orange juice concentrate	1	2	3	4
water	1¾ c	3½ c	6 c	8 c
salt	½ tsp	1 tsp	1¾ tsp	4 tsp
large onions, finely chopped	1	2	4	7
ground turmeric	1 tsp	2 tsp	3¾ tsp	6 tsp
raisins	3 tbs	6 tbs	10 tbs	1½ c
slivered almonds	½ c	1 c	1¾ c	3½ c

In a heavy skillet, melt half the butter and quickly toss the uncooked rice in it. Do not let it brown, but cook just until some of the grains turn white.

Put the rice in a kettle with a tight-fitting lid. Add the orange juice, water, and salt and bring to a boil. Immediately reduce the heat to the lowest possible and let cook, untouched, for 20 minutes. Taste a grain to make sure it is done, then uncover, place a tea towel over the pot, and replace the lid. (This absorbs extra moisture.) Leave the pot off the heat.

Melt the rest of the butter in a heavy skillet. Add the chopped onion and cook, stirring, until golden. Add the turmeric and stir well, then add the raisins and cook for 2 minutes, stirring. Add the almonds, toss, and remove from the heat. Just before serving, toss the rice lightly with the nut mixture.

Eric Widmer's Succotash

This recipe can only be attempted in mid to late summer, when the ingredients are in season. No use trying to make it with frozen or canned vegetables, for its chief virtue lies in its freshness, in the true taste of the beans and corn. It is an unusual succotash, in that it uses fresh shell beans instead of limas.

	6	12	20	50
ears of fresh corn on the cob	5 or 6	10	18	50
		(or more)		
fresh shell beans (the long, red-and-white speckled pods, with reddish beans)	2 lbs	4 lbs	7 lbs	15 lbs
milk, as needed	½ c	1 c	2 c	5 c
salt		(season to taste)		
freshly ground black pepper		(season to taste)		

Shuck the corn, parboil it in a large kettle of boiling water, and run it under cold water. Scrape the kernels from the ears into a saucepan.

Shell the beans, then, in a large kettle of boiling water, cook them at a rolling boil for 15 to 20 minutes. Taste one to see that they are done—they should not be overdone at all, and at this stage it is much better for them to have a slight "bite." Drain them in a colander and then put them in the saucepan with the corn.

Add just enough milk to cook the mixture in—it should not be soupy. Add liberal amounts of salt and freshly ground black pepper. Over a low flame, heat the succotash just until the vegetables are heated through, covered. The succotash should be served in the milk.

NOTE: Butter is optional. This dish should not be made ahead.

Zucchini Casserole

The first tender zucchini of the season need only butter and freshly ground black pepper. The larger, older squash need special treatment, such as the following, to bring out their good qualities.

	6	12	20	50
zucchini, sliced	2½ lbs	5 lbs	8 lbs	17 lbs
large onions, chopped	1	2	4	8
garlic cloves, minced	6	12	20	2½ heads or more
35-oz cans tomatoes, drained and chopped	1	2	4	8
salt		(season to taste)		
freshly ground black pepper		(season to taste)		
granulated sugar	½ tsp	1 tsp	2 tsp	4 tsp
fresh parsley, finely chopped	1 c	2 c	3½ c	5 c
dried oregano	1 tsp	2 tsp	4 tsp	8 tsp
dried basil	1 tsp	2 tsp	4 tsp	8 tsp
olive oil	⅔ c	1⅓ c	2⅔ c	4 c

Combine all the ingredients but the olive oil. Arrange in a broad shallow casserole and pour the olive oil over the top. Bake in a 400° oven for about 50 minutes, or until the oil is bubbling around the zucchini. Serve either hot or at room temperature.

NOTE: This can be successfully reheated.

Uncooked Almond Dessert

This is very rich, almost a marzipan, and should be served in small portions with whipped cream, believe it or not, to "cut" the density.

	6	12	20	50
packages of lady fingers	1	2	4	8
unsalted butter sticks	1	2	4	8
granulated sugar, preferably superfine	½ c	1 c	2 c	4 c
finely ground blanched almonds °	2 c	1½ lbs	2 lbs, 10 ozs	5 lbs, 4 ozs
almond extract	1 tsp	2 tsp	4 tsp	8 tsp
eggs	2	4	8	16

GARNISH

heavy cream	½ pt	1 pt	2 pts	4 pts
candied violets or blanched, slivered almonds				

Separate the ladyfingers and allow them to dry in a very low oven, about 200°, for 10 to 15 minutes. Do not let them brown. Meanwhile, line a small bowl [or 2, 4, or 6 one-quart molds] with long strips of waxed paper, extending over the edges. (These will aid in unmolding the dessert.) Line the bowl [or molds] with ladyfinger halves, saving a few for the top.

In a bowl, cream together the butter and sugar. Mix in the almonds, almond extract, and add the eggs, one at a time, mixing thoroughly after each addition.

° Can be ground in a blender.

Spoon the mixture into the lined bowl [or molds] and top with the reserved ladyfingers. Cover with waxed paper and a small saucer. On the saucer place a heavy object, such as a 1-pound weight, a 2-cup measure filled with water, or parts of a heavy meat grinder. Refrigerate for at least 24 hours. (This may be done 2 or even 3 days ahead.)

Before serving, unmold the dessert onto a cake platter, using the waxed paper strips to help ease it out of the molds. Decorate with the cream, whipped, and candied violets or almonds.

Linzertorte

This nut-pastry jam tart is very rich, so cut it in slivers, rather than slices. It goes very far, and tastes very good.

	6	12	20	50
butter	½ lb	1 lb	1¾ lbs	2½ lbs
granulated sugar	1 c	2 c	3½ c	2 lbs
egg yolks	2	4	7	10
finely ground unblanched almonds	1½ c	1 lb, 2 ozs	1 lb, 14 ozs	3 lbs
lemon rind, grated *	1½ tsp	3 tsp	5 tsp	7½ tsp
all-purpose flour	2 c	4 c	2 lbs, 2 ozs	4 lbs, 4 ozs
ground cinnamon	1 tbs	2 tbs	3 tbs	5 tbs
ground cloves	½ tsp	1 tsp	1¾ tsp	2½ tsp
raspberry preserves	1 c	2 c	3½ c	5 c

Preheat the oven to 350°.

Cream the butter and sugar together, then add the egg yolks and beat well. Stir in the ground almonds and lemon rind. Combine the flour, cinnamon, and cloves and fold into the creamed mixture. Knead until the dough is firm and holds together. [Knead dough in several batches if you are making the larger recipes.]

Pat two-thirds of the dough into a 9-inch round cake pan [2, 3, 5 pans], with removable bottom. The layer should be about ½ inch thick. [For the larger recipes, you can use foil pie pans, if you make sure the layer is flat and uniformly ½ inch thick.] Spread with the preserves.

* One average lemon will yield 2 tablespoons of grated rind.

Roll out the rest of the dough on a table. Cut strips out of the dough (eight strips per pan), and make lattice tops by placing four strips one way, four the other over the preserves and pinching the ends down. Bake for 30 to 40 minutes, then cool. Cut into small pie wedges to serve.

NOTE: Keep in a cool place, tightly covered.

Individual Paris-Brest

While this dessert is traditionally made as a ring, split and filled, it is easier to serve to crowds as individual puffs. Paris-Brest is a kind of cream puff with a rich almond cream filling. While you can make the praline powder and the *crème pralinée* ahead of time, it is necessary to make the puffs on the day of serving. Assemble just before eating, and garnish with whipped cream.

PRALINE POWDER

	6	12	20	50
granulated sugar	¾ c	1½ c	2¾ c	6 c
water	¼ c	½ c	¾ c	1¼ c
cream of tartar	¼ tsp	½ tsp	¾ tsp	1¼ tsp
blanched almonds	½ c	1 c	1½ c	3 c
butter or margarine for greasing pan	1 tbs	2 tbs	3 tbs	5 tbs

CRÈME PRALINÉE

	6	12	20	50
granulated sugar	1 c	2 c	3½ c	7 c
water	⅓ c	⅔ c	1⅓ c	2½ c
cream of tartar	¼ tsp	½ tsp	¾ tsp	1½ tsp
egg yolks, beaten	4	8	12	24
butter, softened	2 sticks	4 sticks	1½ lbs	3 lbs
vanilla extract	2 tsp	4 tsp	6½ tsp	4 tbs
praline powder (above)	½ c	1 c	1¾ c	3½ c

CREAM PUFFS

	6	12	20	50
water	1 c	2 c	3¾ c	8 c
butter	6 tbs	12 tbs	3 sticks	1½ lbs
salt	⅛ tsp	¼ tsp	½ tsp	1 tsp

	6	12	20	50
all-purpose flour	1 c	2 c	3¾ c	2 lbs, 2 ozs
eggs	5	8	15	30
slivered, blanched almonds	¼ c	½ c	1 c	2 c (or 12 ozs)
margarine or shortening for greasing pans	2 tbs	4 tbs	6 tbs	8 tbs
flour	1 tbs	2 tbs	3 tbs	5 tbs

GARNISH

	6	12	20	50
heavy cream	½ pt	1 pt	1½ pts	2 pts

PRALINE POWDER

Combine all of the ingredients for the praline powder in a saucepan and stir over medium heat until the sugar dissolves. Continue to heat, without stirring, until the syrup is dark brown. Watch it carefully, as it burns rapidly at this stage. Pour immediately onto a greased cookie sheet and allow to cool. When cool, break the praline into rough pieces and place, a little at a time, into a blender and blend until powdered. Repeat until all the praline is used. Place in a tightly covered jar until ready to use.

NOTE: Extra praline powder can be frozen or stored for a week or so in the refrigerator.

CRÈME PRALINÉE

Prepare the crème pralinée by combining the sugar, water, and cream of tartar in a heavy saucepan. Bring to a boil, without stirring, and boil until the syrup registers 240° on a candy thermometer. Pour gradually into the egg yolks, beating hard until the mixture is very thick, then, using a whisk or electric beater, add the butter, a little at a time, until the crème is smooth and thick. Add the praline powder and vanilla. Store in the refrigerator until needed.

CREAM PUFFS

When ready to make the cream puffs and assemble the dessert, preheat oven to 450°. Grease and flour cookie sheets.

Place the water, butter, and salt into a saucepan and heat until the butter has melted and the mixture boils. Add the flour all at once and stir over low heat until the mixture forms a ball and leaves the sides of the pan clean.

Remove the pan from heat and beat in 4 [7, 9, 12] of the eggs, one at a time, very well; the mixture should be smooth. Spoon the *chou* paste (as this mixture is called) onto the prepared cookie sheets in 2- to 3-tablespoon amounts. Brush each with the remaining eggs, beaten, and sprinkle almonds on each.

Bake 10 to 15 minutes, until puffed, then lower the heat to 350° and bake for 15 minutes longer. With the point of a knife, or tines of a fork, prick each around the sides and return to the oven to finish baking, around 15 minutes more. Cool on a rack.

ASSEMBLING

Whip the heavy cream.

Just before serving, slice each puff in half horizontally and fill with *crème pralinée*. Replace the top, garnish with the whipped cream, and serve.

Frozen Rum Cream

This is the simplest possible dessert, and yet a great success. Make it in 5-ounce plastic cups for a large group. It can be made 2 or 3 days ahead, if you cover the containers to prevent "freezer smell."

	6	12	20	50
egg yolks	4	8	12	20
granulated sugar	¼ c	½ c	1½ c	2 c
egg whites, beaten stiff	3	6	10	15
heavy cream, whipped until stiff	1½ c	3 c	4½ c	7½ c
rum	½ c	1 c	2½ c	5 c

Beat the egg yolks and sugar together until stiff and lemon colored, then fold in the beaten egg whites and whipped cream and gently stir in the rum. Put into cups or a large bowl and freeze for at least 8 hours.

Fresh Strawberries with Sabayon Sauce

When strawberries are in season, I hate to serve them with anything but sugar, but this sauce is my first choice for a garnish. It is sometimes served warm, but I prefer it chilled.

	6	12	20	50
strawberries, cleaned and hulled	2 pts	4 pts	7 pts	16 pts

S A U C E

	6	12	20	50
egg yolks	4	8	14	32
sugar	½ c	1 c	1¾ c	4 c
heavy cream, whipped	½ pt	1 pt	2 pts	4 pts

Chill the strawberries until serving time.

Place the egg yolks and sugar in the top of a double boiler, or in a large heavy bowl that will fit over a saucepan of simmering water, and beat with a whisk until thick. (Do not overcook or the eggs will scramble.) If lumps form, strain before chilling. Chill.

Just before serving, fold in the whipped cream. Garnish each dish of strawberries with a tablespoon or two of the sauce.

Brandy Alexander Pie

This pie is as sweet and delicious as the drink for which it is named, and a great deal less alcoholic. It is light and fluffy, but very filling.

	6	12	20	50
unflavored gelatin envelopes	**1**	**2**	**4**	**8**
cold water	**½ c**	**1 c**	**2 c**	**4 c**
granulated sugar	**⅔ c**	**1⅓ c**	**2⅔ c**	**2 lbs**
salt	**⅛ tsp**	**¼ tsp**	**½ tsp**	**1 tsp**
eggs, separated	**3**	**6**	**12**	**24**
Cognac	**¼ c**	**½ c**	**1 c**	**2 c**
Grand Marnier	**¼ c**	**½ c**	**1 c**	**2 c**
or				
crème de cacao	**¼ c**	**½ c**	**1 c**	**2 c**
heavy cream	**2 c**	**4 c**	**4 pts**	**8 pts**
9-inch graham cracker crust	**1**	**2**	**4**	**8**

GARNISH

four-ounce bars semisweet chocolate	**1**	**2**	**2½**	**3**
cream	**1 c**	**2 c**	**3½ c**	**6 c**

Sprinkle the gelatin over the cold water in a saucepan. Add ⅓ cup [⅔ cup, 1⅓ cups, 2⅔ cups] of the sugar, the salt, and egg yolks. Stir to blend, then heat over low heat, stirring, until the gelatin dissolves and the mixture thickens. Do not boil. Remove from the heat and stir in the Cognac and Grand Marnier (or crème de cacao). Chill in the refrigerator until the mixture mounds slightly and is thick.

Beat the egg whites until stiff (use a portable electric mixer in a large kettle). Gradually beat in the remaining sugar and fold into the thickened mixture. Whip half of the cream until it holds peaks. Fold in the whipped cream, and turn into the crusts. Chill several hours, or overnight. To serve, garnish with the remaining cream, whipped. Using a vegetable peeler, make chocolate curls from the chocolate bars and let drop onto the cream.

Kulfi

This frozen Indian dessert is something like our ice cream, but with an exotic character, very rich and sensuous, all its own. It is good also with Middle Eastern meals. Since it melts very rapidly when removed from the freezer, take it out just before you serve it.

Rosewater is available in Middle Eastern, Indian, and specialty markets or in some pharmacies. It makes this dessert exotic.

	6	12	20	50
13-oz cans sweetened condensed milk	1	2	4	8
heavy cream	1 c	2 c	4 c	8 c
rosewater	½ tsp	1 tsp	2 tsp	4 tsp
or				
vanilla extract	½ tsp	1 tsp	2 tsp	4 tsp
almonds, finely chopped (not ground in blender)	¼ c	½ c	1 c	2 c
pistachio nuts, finely chopped	¼ c	½ c	1 c	2 c

Mix all the ingredients together, stir well, and freeze. For a small party, you can freeze it in a dessert bowl, or in individual plastic cups. [For a large group, I freeze it in disposable, clear, 5-ounce plastic cups.] During the freezing, which takes 4 hours or more, the nuts rise to the top.

Fyrste Kake

This is a Norwegian cake, which is very rich and almondy. Serve it in very thin wedges, with fresh strawberries or blueberries. Add whipped cream if you like.

	6	12	20	50
unsalted butter	¾ c	1½ c	1½ lbs	3 lbs
granulated sugar	1¾ c	3½ c	2⅝ lbs	5 lbs, 4 ozs
eggs, separated	3	6	10	18
all-purpose flour	2½ c plus 2 tbs	5 c plus 4 tbs	2 lbs, 13 ozs plus 7 tbs	5 lbs plus ¾ c
baking powder	3 tsp	6 tsp	10 tsp	6 tbs
almond extract	1½ tsp	3 tsp	5 tsp	8 tsp
ground, blanched almonds	1 c	2 c	3½ c	6 c

Preheat the oven to 350°.

Cream together the butter and ¾ cup [1½ cups, 2¾ cups, 4½ cups] of the sugar. Add the yolks of the eggs, one at a time, beating well after each addition. Stir in the 2½ cups [5 cups, 2 lbs 13 oz, 5 lbs] flour and the baking powder. Add 1 teaspoon [2 teaspoons, 3½ teaspoons, 5 teaspoons] of the almond extract.

Reserve ½ cup [1 cup, 1¾ cup, 3 cups] of the dough for the topping and spread the remaining dough over the bottom of a greased 9-inch cake pan [2 pans, 4 pans, 6 pans].

Beat the egg whites until frothy and gradually add the remaining cup [2 cups, 4¾ cups, 6 cups] sugar, beating constantly until stiff.

[For large amounts, use a hand-held beater in a large kettle.] Fold in the almonds and the remaining ½ teaspoon [1 teaspoon, 1½ teaspoons, 3 teaspoons] almond extract. Spread this filling over the lined cake pans.

Add the remaining 2 tablespoons [4 tablespoons, 7 tablespoons, ¾ cup] flour to the reserved dough. Roll out on a floured board, cut into strips, and lay the strips in a crisscross pattern on top of the almond mixture. Bake for 45 to 50 minutes, then cool and serve in thin slices with berries and cream.

NOTE: Keep in a cool place, tightly covered.

Baklava

Layers of paper-thin, crispy pastry alternated with ground nuts and soaked in a honey syrup make this dessert a treat. *Baklava* is a simple assembly job when you buy frozen or fresh phyllo dough. And it never fails to impress! It's almost a shame to have to say you didn't make the phyllo.

Phyllo is a paper-thin pastry "leaf" that is used for *baklava, spanokopita,* and many other Middle Eastern dishes. It can be bought at Greek or Middle Eastern groceries or at specialty shops. It is often sold frozen, wrapped in plastic, and should be defrosted overnight, in its own wrapper, in the refrigerator. Since it becomes brittle and unworkable quickly when exposed to air, you should keep it covered with a layer of waxed paper covered with a very slightly damp cloth as you work, but don't let it get *wet,* or it will stick together.

PASTRY

	12	50
shelled almonds, walnuts, or pecans, or a mixture	2 c	8 c
granulated sugar	2 tbs	½ c
ground cinnamon	½ tsp	1 tsp
butter	½ lb	1½ lbs
phyllo dough	1 lb	4 lbs

SYRUP

	12	50
granulated sugar	2 c	6 c
water	2 c	6 c
strips of lemon rind, ½ inch by 3 inches	2	6
cinnamon stick (optional)	1	3
honey	½ c	1½ c

Chop the nuts fine. (You can use a blender, but it pulverizes them, so leave out some to chop for texture.) Add the sugar and ground cinnamon to the nuts and set aside. Melt the butter in a small pan and set aside.

Combine all the syrup ingredients except the honey in a saucepan and bring to a boil. Boil for 5 minutes, then remove the rinds and sticks. Add the honey and set aside.

Preheat the oven to 375°. In large roasting pan [or two], spread five or six layers of phyllo, brushing each with melted butter, then sprinkle a handful of the nut mixture on top of the last layer. Continue to layer, brushing butter on each and sprinkling nuts on each. The last five or six layers should be brushed with butter only. End with one perfect layer.

Before baking, cut into small diamonds (about 2 inches) with a very sharp knife.

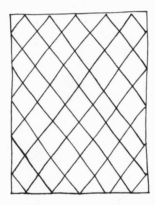

Pour about ½ cup of the remaining butter over all and bake at 375° for 30 minutes, then lower the heat to 350° for 30 more minutes, or until the *baklava* is golden brown.

Remove from the oven and immediately pour the cooled syrup over the *baklava;* it will be absorbed into the pastry. Let cool.

NOTE: *Baklava* will keep refrigerated for about a week, but is best in the first 2 or 3 days.

Biscuit Tortoni

Biscuit tortoni is like a frozen mousse, but richer and more interesting in texture. You can add rum instead of vanilla, if you prefer. This is my favorite frozen dessert.

	6	12	20	50
granulated sugar	⅜ c	¾ c	1½ c	3 c
water	⅜ c	¾ c	1½ c	3 c
eggs, separated	2	4	8	16
almond macaroons	6	12	24	48
almond extract	1 tsp	1½ tsp	3 tsp	6 tsp
vanilla extract	1 tsp	1½ tsp	3 tsp	6 tsp
heavy cream	1 c	2 c	4 c	8 c

Combine the sugar and water in a saucepan and cook, without stirring, until the mixture reads 230° on a candy thermometer.

In a very large bowl, beat the egg whites until stiff. Slowly stir the sugar syrup into the egg whites and mix well. In another bowl, beat the egg yolks until thick and pale, and fold into egg white mixture, stirring well.

Pulverize the macaroons in a blender, or crumble them into fine crumbs between your fingers. Keep out 3 tablespoons [6 tablespoons, ½ cup, ¾ cup] for the garnish and add the rest to the mixture. Add the almond and vanilla extracts.

Whip the cream until stiff. Fold carefully and thoroughly into the mixture [by this time, the amounts will be enormous, so I find it best to use a big preserving kettle to mix the cream and egg mix-ture together], then sprinkle the reserved macaroon crumbs on top, and freeze in individual cups.[I use clear plastic, disposable, 5-ounce cups for a crowd.]

NOTE: This can be made 2 to 3 days ahead, if kept covered and placed in a reliable freezer.

Almond Cheesecake

This is a surprisingly sophisticated cheesecake, though just as rich and filling as any. Each cake will serve at least ten. The large amount makes five cakes.

	10	50
granulated sugar	1 c less 2 tbs	4 c plus 6 tbs
butter, left at room temperature to soften	4 tbs	2½ sticks
cream cheese, left at room temperature to soften for 3 hours	1 lb	5 lbs
all-purpose flour	¼ c	1¼ c
honey	2 tbs	1 c plus 2 tbs
eggs, separated	5	25
light cream	½ c	2½ c
almond extract	¼ tsp	1¼ tsp
vanilla	1 tsp	5 tsp
almonds, pulverized in blender	½ c	2½ c
light brown sugar	¼ c	1¼ c
ground cinnamon	1 tsp	5 tsp
almonds, finely chopped (not pulverized in blender)	¼ c	1¼ c

Preheat the oven to 325°. Grease and flour one [2, 3, 5] spring form pans or straight-sided 1½-inch-deep cake tins.

Cream the sugar and butter together, then add the cream cheese and beat until fluffy. Add the flour, honey, and egg yolks and beat well. Add the light cream and extracts. Beat the egg whites until stiff and fold them into the sugar and butter, then fold in the pulverized almonds and pour into the pans.

Combine the brown sugar, cinnamon, and chopped almonds and sprinkle over the batter. Bake for 1 hour at 325°, then allow to cool in the oven for about 2 hours. Chill (although this is best served at room temperature).

NOTE: This can be made 1 or 2 days ahead.

Brandied Fruit Cup

This list of fruits is only a suggestion for a change from the ordinary fruit cocktail. You should really invent your own combination. The following is a successful one, based on dried fruit, and is especially good during seasons when fresh fruits are hard to get.

	6	12	20	50
5-oz packages dried apricots	1	2	3	5
mixed dried fruits, 12-oz boxes	1	2	3	5
20-oz cans Queen Anne cherries	1	2	3	5
fresh or canned Bing cherries	1 lb	2 lbs	3 lbs	5 lbs
grapefruit	1	2	3	5
8-oz jars preserved kumquats	½	1	2	4
11-oz cans mandarin oranges	1	2	4	8
20-oz jars figs in syrup	1	2	3	5
bananas	3	6	10	25
strawberries, blueberries, or any fruit in season	(as available)			
Cognac or kirsch	(to taste)			
superfine, granulated sugar	(to taste)			

Place all the dried fruits in a saucepan with water to cover. Simmer for about 20 minutes, or until tender. Let cool in the liquid.

Pit anything that has pits. Peel and cut the oranges and grapefruit into bite-sized chunks. Cut the cooled dried fruits into small pieces. Use the syrup from only one of the canned fruits (fig is nice) and drain the other canned fruits.

Combine all the fruits in a large bowl and add sugar and Cognac to taste. (For a non-alcoholic cup, add lemon juice or apricot nectar or a little cranberry juice.)

Serve with Butter Nutball Cookies on page 168.

NOTE: This is best made in the morning for evening serving, or the day before if for luncheon. It can be kept, unrefrigerated, in a cool place.

Butter Nutball Cookies

These—buttery, nutty, sugary—are irresistible. I serve fruit cup or ice cream just as an excuse to make these.

	4 dozen
all-purpose flour	2 c
granulated sugar	½ c
salt	½ tsp
butter, or butter and margarine, mixed	½ lb
vanilla extract	2 tsp
finely chopped walnuts or pecans, not pulverized in blender	2 c

GARNISH

confectioner's sugar

Preheat the oven to 350°

Mix all the ingredients except the confectioners' sugar together in a large bowl. [I use the preserving kettle and my hands.] Form into small balls the size of walnuts and place on cookie sheets an inch apart. Bake at 350° until set (about 15 minutes; they will not brown. While they are still warm, but not just out of the oven, roll each in confectioner's sugar and let cool without stacking them.

NOTE: For serving to 50, with a fruit cup or ice cream, double all the amounts, which will yield about 2 cookies per person.

Charlotte Malakoff au Chocolat

This is my favorite dessert of all, the most voluptuous combination of chocolate, liqueur, almonds, butter, and cream. For a time when only pleasure matters.

	10	50
orange liqueur (Grand Marnier or Cointreau)	½ c	2¼ c
water	⅓ c	2 c
ladyfingers	18–20	100 or so
unsalted butter, softened	1½ sticks	2½ lbs
superfine, granulated sugar	¾ c	5 c
almond extract	¼ tsp	1¼ tsp
semisweet chocolate melted in	3 ozs	20 ozs
strong coffee	½ c	1¼ c
ground almonds	1 c	6⅔ c
heavy cream	1½ c	5 pts

Combine ¼ cup [1 cup] of the orange liqueur with the water. Separate the ladyfingers and dip, one by one, in the water-liqueur mixture. Place on cake racks to drain. Meanwhile, line the bottom of a 1½-quart mold [or five of them] with waxed paper. Line sides of the molds with ladyfingers, standing them on end. Reserve the remaining ladyfingers.

Cream the butter and sugar together until light and fluffy. Beat in the remaining orange liqueur and the almond extract and continue to beat for five minutes. Fold in the chocolate, then add the almonds.

Whip the cream until it reaches the "chantilly" stage, that is, until it holds its shape when a spoon is drawn across the surface. Fold the cream into the almond mixture, then pour the mixture into the molds, layering with the remaining ladyfingers, and ending with a layer of ladyfingers.

Cover with a round of waxed paper and place a saucer over the mixture. Put some heavy weight on the saucer—pieces of a meat grinder, a 1-pound scale weight, a heavy can—and refrigerate overnight. Unmold before serving and, if desired, serve with whipped cream.

NOTE: These may be made two days ahead.

Lemon Mousse

Lemon is a particularly good flavor with which to end a meal, especially a spicy one. It alerts the sodden senses, and leaves a pleasant astringency. This one is quite easy to prepare.

MOUSSE

	6	12	20	50
lemons	2	4	7	15
eggs, separated	4	8	14	32
granulated sugar	¼ c	½ c	¾ c	2 c
envelopes gelatin, unflavored	1	2	3½	8
heavy cream	¾ c	1½ c	2¼ c	6 c

GARNISH

	6	12	20	50
heavy cream, to whip	1 c	2 c	3 c	5 c
toasted, slivered almonds	½ c	1 c	1¾ c	3 c

Grate the rinds of the lemons (yellow part only) and set aside. Squeeze the juice and reserve it. Combine the egg yolks with the reserved rind and sugar. Beat hard until the mixture is light and lemon colored.

Combine the lemon juice and gelatin and let stand for 10 minutes, then heat the mixture over low heat or hot water until the gelatin dissolves. Stir into the yolk mixture.

Beat the cream until thick and fold into the mousse mixture. Whip the egg whites until stiff, then fold in to the mousse mixture. For 6, pour into a soufflé dish and chill. [For 50, chill in 5-ounce plastic disposable cups.] Before serving, top with the whipped cream and almonds.

Nepali Fruit Dahi

This is a fresh fruit and spiced yogurt mixture, one of the few desserts served, aside from plain fruit, after a Nepali meal. The fruits suggested aren't compulsory; you can make substitutions. Nepali oranges are like tangerines, which are actually better in this dish anyway.

	6	12	20	50
coconuts	½	1	2	3
ripe pineapples	1	2	2	3
or				
20-oz cans pineapple				
chunks	1	2	3	6
bananas	2	4	7	12
oranges	3	6	10	20
fresh strawberries	1 pt	1 qt	1 qt plus 1 pt	2 qts
raw cashews or raw peanuts				
(don't use salted)	½ lb	1 lb	1¾ lbs	4 lbs
plain yogurt	2 pts	4 pts	6 pts	4 qts
seeds from cardamom pods, smashed with a mortar and pestle	4 pods	8 pods	12 pods	15 pods
superfine granulated sugar or raw sugar, if available		(to taste)		

Make holes in the coconut and drain out the milk; reserve it for other uses. (It makes a good liquid for cooking curries.) Put the coconut, in a preheated 400° oven for 5 to 10 minutes. (This helps in the removal of the skin.) Crack the coconut open with a hammer and peel the brown skin off the meat with a parer or sharp knife. Cut the coconut meat into small ¼-inch chunks and put in a bowl with water to cover.

Peel and dice the pineapple into ½-inch chunks. Place in large bowl along with the bananas, sliced; the oranges, cut in ½-inch chunks; and the strawberries, washed, hulled, and halved. Add the coconut and raw nuts and toss lightly.

Combine the yogurt, cardamom, cinnamon, and sugar to taste. Mix the yogurt lightly with the fruit, and chill before serving.

Toasted Almond Parfait

This is a terribly easy assembly job. If you make it in clear cups, it's an attractive frozen dessert. Very good for large groups, and well liked by children if you leave out the rum. You may want to use blended syrup, as pure maple is expensive. Do *not* use "maple-flavoring."

	6	12	20	50
6-oz packages unblanched almonds	1	2	3½	8
maple syrup	¾ c	1½ c	2¾ c	6 c
rum (optional)	2 tbs	4 tbs	7 tbs	1 c
vanilla ice cream, softened	2 pts	2 qts	3½ qts	8 qts

GARNISH

heavy cream, to be whipped	1 c	2 c	3 c	5 c

Preheat the oven to 400°.

Spread the almonds on a baking sheet and toast in the oven, turning occasionally, until browned. Do not let them burn. Chop very fine with food chopper (*not* in the blender). Mix the almonds with the maple syrup to make a thin paste, adding the rum if desired.

Spoon a generous tablespoon of almond paste into the bottom of each of six parfait glasses [or 5-ounce disposable plastic cups]. Cover with a layer of ice cream. Continue the layers until the cups are full; then cover with plastic wrap and freeze until hard. Thirty minutes before serving, remove from the freezer and put in the refrigerator. Top with whipped cream.

Illustrations

Two ways to improvise a steamer — xv

Folding Momos — 9

Baking paté — 24

Weighting paté — 24

Steaming Couscous — 63

Rolling Roulades Piquantes — 91

Stuffing cabbage — 93

Cutting Baklava — 162

Index

A

almonds
  charlotte Malakoff au chocolat, 169–170
  cheesecake, 165
  dessert, uncooked, 147–148
  fyrste kake, 159–160
  kulfi, 158
  linzertorte, 149–150
  orange rice pilaf, 141
  parfait, toasted, 174
  Paris-Brest, 151–153
appetizers and first courses
  baba g'hanouj, 15
  chopped chicken livers, Phyllis Blumberg's, 20
  crabmeat pastry, 5–6
  dolmathis, 16–17
  homous, 14
  momos, 7–10
  Moroccan chermoulah, 13
  pâté de campagne, 23–24
  quiches, 18–19
  salad méchouia, 11–12
  shrimp
    in dill pesto, 4
    New Orleans, 3
  Sicilian broccoli, 123
  see also soup
apricots
  brandied fruit cup, 166–167
artichokes
  and chicken (pollo alla limone), 77–78
  and chick-peas vinaigrette, 128

B

baba g'hanouj, 15
baklava, 161–162
bananas
  brandied fruit cup, 166–167
  Nepali fruit dahi, 172–173
  raita, 135
beans, kidney, *see* kidney beans
beans, shell
  Eric Widmer's succotash, 142
bean sprout salad, 124
béchamel sauce, 89
beef
  borscht, Putney School, 49–50
  carbonnades flamandes, 110–111
  chili, Joy Walker's, 69–70
  cocida Valenciana, 114–115
  dirty rice, 112–113
  lasagne, 108–109
  meatballs
    Swedish, 81–82
    sweet, 66–67
  momos, 7–10
  moussaka, 87–88
  nasi goreng, 95–96
  ragoût, 75–76
  roulades piquantes, 90–91
  spaghetti sauce, 101–102
  stifatho, 106–107
beets
  Putney School borscht, 49–50
biscuit tortoni, 163–164
Blumberg, Phyllis
  chopped chicken livers, 20
borscht, Putney School, 49–50
bouquet garni, 110
brandied fruit cup, 166–167
brandy Alexander pie, 156–157
bread
  pumpernickel, 21–22
  Swedish limpa, 25–26
  Syrian (pita), 11
bread crumbs
  to make, 125

broccoli
  Sicilian, 123
  soup, 31
bulghur wheat salad (tabbouleh),
    132
butter, clarified, 139
Butterfield, Ellen
  dolmathis, 16–17
butter nutball cookies, 168

C

cabbage, stuffed, 92–94
cakes
  almond cheesecake, 165
  fyrste kake, 159–160
carbonnades flamandes, 110–111
cashews
  Nepali fruit dahi, 172–173
cauliflower soup, 37–38
Chao, Phebe
  Chinese spiced eggplant, 121–
    122
charlotte Malakoff au chocolat, 169–
    170
Cheddar cheese
  chilaquiles, 53–54
  green enchiladas, 98–99
cheese
  Cheddar
    chilaquiles, 53–54
    green enchiladas, 98–99
  cream
    almond cheesecake, 165
  farmer's
    spanokopita, 47–48
  feta
    beef stifatho, 106–107
    with shrimp, 51–52
    spanokopita, 47–48
  mozzarella
    lasagne, 108–109
  Parmesan
    chicken Parisienne, 59–60
    moussaka, 88
    pesto, 103
  ricotta

lasagne, 108–109
Romano
  chicken Parisienne, 59–60
  lasagne, 108–109
Swiss
  quiche, 18–19
cheesecake, almond, 165
cherries
  brandied fruit cup, 166–167
chermoulah, Moroccan, 13
chicken
  Bengal, 61–62
  broth, 53
  chilaquiles, 53–54
  livers
    cabbage, stuffed, 92–94
    pâté de campagne, 23–24
    Phyllis Blumberg's, 20
  nasi goreng, 95–96
  paprikash, 57–58
  Parisienne, 59–60
  pâté de campagne, 23–24
  pollo al Jerez, 85–86
  pollo alla limone, 77–78
  soup, Senegalese, 42–43
  tandoori, 55–56
chick-peas
  and artichokes vinaigrette, 128
  homous, 14
  Portuguese sausage casserole, 73–
    74
chilaquiles, 53–54
chili, Joy Walker's, 69–70
chili paste, 121
chili peppers, see peppers, hot
Chinese noodles with meat sauce,
    104–105
Chinese spiced eggplant, 121–122
chocolate
  charlotte Malakoff au chocolat,
    169–170
  pumpernickel bread, 21–22
chutney, kishmish, 134
clam chowder, New England, 35–
    36
clarified butter, 139
cocida Valenciana, 114–115

cold cucumber soup, 29
conversion table, xx
cookies, butter nutball, 168
cooking time, x
coriander ("cilantro," "Chinese pars-
    ley"), 69
corn
    Eric Widmer's succotash, 142
couscous, xv, 63–65
    sweet meatballs, 66–67
crabmeat pastry, 5–6
cracked wheat salad (tabbouleh),
    132
cream cheese
    almond cheesecake, 165
cream of mushroom soup, 27–28
cream puffs, 151–152, 153
crème pralinée, 151, 152
Crespo, Vicente de
    cocida Valenciana, 114–115
cucumber
    raita, 135–136
    soup
        cold, 29
        and yogurt"
curries
    chicken Bengal, 61–62
    with kishmish chutney, 134
    lamb (rogan jaush), 79–80
    lentil (dhal), 139–140
    with orange rice pilaf, 141
    pork vindaloo, 71–72
    with raitas, 135–136
curry powder, 61

D

dashi, 83
desserts
    almond cheesecake, 165
    almond, uncooked, 147–148
    almond parfait, toasted, 174
    baklava, 161–162
    biscuit tortoni, 163–164
    brandied fruit cup, 166–167
    brandy Alexander pie, 156–157

butter nutball cookies, 168
charlotte Malakoff au chocolat,
    169–170
fyrste kake, 159–160
kulfi, 158
lemon mousse, 171
linzertorte, 149–150
Nepali fruit dahi, 172–173
Paris-Brest, 151–153
rum cream, frozen, 154
strawberries with sabayon sauce,
    155
dhal, 139–140
dill pesto, 4
dirty rice, 112–113
dolmathis, 16–17
dumplings, see momos

E

egg pancakes, 96
eggplant
    baba g'hanouj, 15
    Chinese spiced, 121–122
    moussaka, 87–88
    ratatouille, 126–127
enchiladas, green, 98–99
Eric Widmer's succotash, 142

F

farmer's cheese
    spanokopita, 47–48
fermented watercress soup, 39
feta cheese
    beef stifatho, 106–107
    with shrimp, 51–52
    spanokopita, 47–48
figs
    brandied fruit cup, 166–167
fox noodles, 83–84
French dressing, 3
    with garlic, 130
frozen rum cream, 154
fruit cup, brandied, 166–167
fruit dahi, Nepali, 172–173
fyrste kake, 159–160

G

garlic
  to peel, 32
  French dressing, 130
  soup, 32–33
ghee, 139
Glaude, Gladys, 112
  dirty rice, 112–113
goulash, *see* szekely gulyas
grapefruit
  brandied fruit cup, 166–167
grape leaves, stuffed (dolmathis),
    16–17
green enchiladas, 98–99

H

ham
  roulades piquantes, 90–91
harissa, 11, 63
hearty spaghetti sauce, 101–102
herbs, xviii
  bouquet garni, 110
hoisin sauce, 104
homous, 14

I

ice cream
  toasted almond parfait, 174

J

Joy Walker's chili, 69–70

K

kidney beans, red
  Joy Walker's chili, 69–70
kidney beans, white
  Portuguese sausage casserole, 73–
    74
kishmish chutney, 134
kulfi, 158
kumquats
  brandied fruit cup, 166–167

L

lamb
  couscous, 63–65
  moussaka, 87–88
  rogan jaush, 79–80
  sweet meatballs, 66–67
lapin chasseur, 68
lasagne, 108–109
legumes, *see* chick-peas; kidney
    beans; lentils
lemons
  and chicken (pollo alla limone),
    77–78
  mousse, 171
lentils
  dhal, 139–140
  soup with mettwurst, 40–41
limpa bread, Swedish, 25–26
linzertorte, 149–150

M

measurements
  conversion table, xx
  for spices, x, xi
meat, *see individual meats*
meatballs
  Swedish, 81–82
  sweet, 66–67
méchouia, salad, 11–12
mirch, Kashmiri, 55
momos, xv, 7–10
Moroccan chermoulah, 13
moussaka, 87–89
mousse, lemon, 171
mozzarella cheese
  lasagne, 108–109
mushrooms
  cream of mushroom soup, 27–28
  hearty spaghetti sauce, 101–102
mustard oil, 7n

N

nasi goreng, 95–96
Nepali fruit dahi, 172–173

New England clam chowder, 35–36
New Orleans shrimp, 3
noodles
  chicken Parisienne, 59–60
  Chinese, with meat sauce, 104–105
  fox, 83–84

O

olive oil, 130n
onions
  to peel, 85n, 116
  quiche, 18–19
  ratatouille, 126–127
  salad, with oranges and cress, 129
oranges
  brandied fruit cup, 166–167
  Nepali fruit dahi, 172–173
  rice pilaf, 141
  salad, with red onions and cress, 129

P

pachadi, tomato, 137
pancakes
  egg, 96
  green enchiladas, 98–99
paprika
  Hungarian, 55, 57
  Spanish, 55
paprikash, chicken, 57–58
parfait, toasted almond, 174
Paris-Brest, 151–153
Parmesan cheese
  chicken Parisienne, 59–60
  moussaka, 88
  pesto, 103
pasta, *see* lasagne; noodles; spaghetti
pastry
  cream puffs, 151–152, 153
  phyllo
    baklava, 161–162
    with crabmeat, 5–6

with spinach (spanokopita), 47–48
  tarts (linzertorte), 149–150
pâté de campagne, 23–24
pavo estofado, 116–117
peanuts
  Nepali fruit dahi, 172–173
pecans
  baklava, 161–162
  butter nutball cookies, 168
peppers, hot
  to clean, 53n
  chicken Bengal, 61–62
  chicken tandoori, 55–56
  chilaquiles, 53–54
  chili, Joy Walker's, 69–70
  Chinese spiced eggplant, 121–122
  couscous, 63–65
  green enchiladas, 98–99
  momos, 7–10
  pork vindaloo, 71–72
  rogan jaush, 79–80
  salad méchouia, 11–12
  tomato pachadi, 137
peppers, sweet
  Chinese spiced eggplant, 121–122
  Moroccan chermoulah, 13
  ratatouille, 126–127
  salad méchouia, 11–12
  spaghetti sauce, 101–102
pesto, 103
  dill, 4
Phyllis Blumberg's chopped chicken livers, 20
phyllo (pastry)
  baklava, 161–162
  with crabmeat, 5–6
  with spinach (spanokopita), 47–48
pie, brandy Alexander, 156–157
pilaf, orange rice, 141
pineapple
  Nepali fruit dahi, 172–173
pita, 11
pollo al Jerez, 85–86

pollo alla limone, 77–78
pork
cabbage, stuffed, 92–94
meat sauce, 104–105
momos, 7–10
pâté de campagne, 23–24
roulades piquantes, 90–91
Swedish meatballs, 81–82
szekely gulyas, 100
vindaloo, 71–72
see also sausage
Portuguese sausage casserole, 73–74
potatoes
achar, 138
Putney School borscht, 49–50
spinach soup, 34
watercress soup, fermented, 39
pots, pans, and utensils, x, xiv
steamer, improvised, xv, 63
praline powder, 151, 152
prunes
pavo estofado, 116–117
sweet meatballs, 66–67
pumpernickel bread, 21–22
Putney School borscht, 49–50

Q

quiches, 18–19

R

rabbit stew (lapin chasseur), 68
ragoût, beef, 75–76
raisins
kishmish chutney, 134
orange rice pilaf, 141
raita
banana, 135
cucumber, 135–136
rice
cabbage, stuffed, 92–94
dirty, 112–113
herbed, in dolmathis, 16–17
orange pilaf, 141
salad, 133

ricotta cheese
lasagne, 108–109
Romano cheese
chicken Parisienne, 59–60
lasagne, 108–109
rosewater, 158
roulades piquantes, 90–91

S

sabayon sauce, 155
salad dressings
French (vinaigrette), 3
garlic, 130
salads
artichokes and chick-peas vinaigrette, 128
bean sprouts, 124
greens, preparation of, xv, 129
méchouia, 11–12
orange-red onion-cress, 129
rice, 133
tabbouleh, 132
sauces
béchamel, 89
meat, 104–105
pesto, 103
dill, 4
sabayon, 155
tomato
canned, 87
fresh, 89
hearty spaghetti, 101–102
spicy, 7, 8, 9–10
vinaigrette (French), 3
garlic, 130
sauerkraut
cabbage, stuffed, 92–94
szekely gulyas, 100
sausage
Chinese, with fox noodles, 83–84
with lentil soup, 40–41
Portuguese casserole, 73–74
seafood
crabmeat pastry, 5–6

seafood (*continued*)
  clam chowder, New England, 35–36
  shrimp
    bean sprout salad, 124
    in dill pesto, 4
    with feta cheese, 51–52
    nasi goreng, 95–96
    New Orleans, 3
    quiche, 18–19
  tuna (salad méchouia), 11–12
Senegalese soup, 42–43
sesame oil, 95, 121
sesame paste (tahini)
  and chick-peas (homous), 14
  and eggplant (baba g'hanouj), 15
sesame seeds
  broccoli soup, 31
Shi, Mr.
  fermented watercress soup, 39
shrimp
  bean sprout salad, 124
  in dill pesto, 4
  with feta cheese, 51–52
  nasi goreng, 95–96
  New Orleans, 3
  quiche, 18–19
Sicilian broccoli, 123
soup
  borscht, Putney School, 49–50
  broccoli, 31
  cauliflower, 37–38
  chicken broth, 53
  clam chowder, New England, 35–36
  cocido Valenciana, broth, 114–115
  cucumber
    cold, 29
    and yogurt, 135–136
  garlic, 32–33
  lentil, with mettwurst, 40–41
  mushroom, cream of, 27–28
  Senegalese, 42–43
  spinach, 34
  watercress, fermented, 39

soybean curd (tofu)
  fox noodles, 83–84
soy sauce, 95n
spaghetti
  sauce
    meat, 104–105
    pesto, 103
    tomato, 101–102
  and soybean curd, 83–84
spanokopita, 47–48
spices, xviii, xix
  measurement, x, xi
spinach
  quiche, 18–19
  soup, 34
  spanokopita, 47–48
squash, *see* zucchini
stews
  beef ragoût, 75–76
  beef stifatho, 106–107
  carbonnades flamandes, 110–111
  lapin chasseur, 68
  ratatouille, 126–127
stifatho, beef, 106–107
strawberries
  brandied fruit cup, 166–167
  Nepali fruit dahi, 172–173
  with sabayon sauce, 155
stuffed cabbage, 92–94
Swedish limpa bread, 25–26
Swedish meatballs, 81–82
sweet meatballs, 66–67
Swiss cheese
  quiche, 18–19
Syrian bread (pita), 11
szekely gulyas, 100

T

tabbouleh, 132
tahini
  and chick-peas (homous), 14
  and eggplant (baba g'hanouj), 15
tandoori, chicken, 55–56
toasted almond parfait, 174
tofu
  fox noodles, 83–84

tomatoes
  to peel, 51
  beef stifatho, 106–107
  cabbage, stuffed, 92–94
  chilaquiles, 53–54
  chili, Joy Walker's, 69–70
  garlic soup, 32–33
  kishmish chutney, 134
  pachadi, 137
  pollo al Jerez, 85–86
  pork vindaloo, 71–72
  Portuguese sausage casserole, 73–74
  Provençale, 125
  ratatouille, 126–127
  rogan jaush, 79–80
  salad méchouia, 11–12
  sauce
    canned, 87
    fresh, 89
    hearty spaghetti, 101–102
    spicy, 7, 8, 9–10
  shrimp with feta cheese, 51–52
  and zucchini, casserole, 143
tuna salad (méchouia), 11–12
turkey
  pavo estofado, 16–17

U

uncooked almond dessert, 147–148

V

veal
  pâté de campagne, 23–24
  Swedish meatballs, 81–82
vegetables
  garlic soup, 32–33
  quiches, 18–19
  raita, 135–136
  ratatouille, 126–127
  see also individual vegetables
vinaigrette dressing, 3
  garlic, 130

W

Walker, Joy
  chili, 69–70
walnuts
  baklava, 161–162
  butter nutball cookies, 168
watercress
  salad, with oranges and red onions, 129
  soup, fermented, 39
Widmer, Eric
  succotash, 142
Williams, Louella, 112
  green enchiladas, 98–99
working area, xiv
  for salads, xv, 129

Y

Yarborough, Trin
  cocida Valenciana, 114–115
yogurt
  banana raita, 135
  cucumber raita, 135–136
  and cucumber soup, 30
  Nepali fruit dahi, 172–173

Z

zucchini
  ratatouille, 126–127
  and tomatoes, casserole, 143